SOCIAL WORK

Series Editor: Jo Campling

BASW

Social work is at an important stage in its development. All professions must be responsive to changing social and economic conditions if they are to meet the needs of those they serve. This series focuses on sound practice and the specific contribution which social workers can make to the well-being of our society in the 1980s.

The British Association of Social Workers has always been conscious of its role in setting guidelines for practice and in seeking to raise professional standards. The conception of the Practical Social Work series arose from a survey of BASW members to discover where they, the practitioners in social work, felt there was the most need for new literature. The response was overwhelming and enthusiastic, and the result is a carefully planned, coherent series of books. The emphasis is firmly on practice, set in a theoretical framework. The books will inform, stimulate and promote discussion, thus adding to the further development of skills and high professional standards. All the authors are practitioners and teachers of social work, representing a wide variety of experience.

JO CAMPLING

PRACTICAL SOCIAL WORK

Series Editor: Jo Campling

BASW

PUBLISHED

Working in Teams
Malcolm Payne

Social Work with the Dying and Bereaved
Carole R. Smith

Community Work
Alan Twelvetrees

FORTHCOMING

Social Work and Mental Handicap
David Anderson

Residential Social Work
Roger Clough

Social Work with Ethnic Minorities
Alun Jackson

Social Work Skills with Old People
Mary Marshall

Social Work with the Disabled
Michael Oliver

Social Work with the Mentally Ill
Colin Pritchard and Alan Butler

Social Work with Juvenile Offenders
David Thorpe, Norman Tutt, David Smith and
Christopher Green

Social Work with the Dying and Bereaved

Carole R. Smith

First published 1982 by
THE MACMILLAN PRESS LTD
London and Basingstoke
Companies and representatives throughout the world

ISBN 0 333 30894 8 (hard cover)
ISBN 0 333 30895 6 (paper cover)

Typeset in Great Britain by
STYLESET LIMITED
Salisbury · Wiltshire

Printed in Hong Kong

To my mother and grandmother — with love and many thanks

Contents

1 **Setting the Scene**   1

  Introduction   1
  The issues   3

2 **Knowledge about Dying: the Data**   10

  A few words about knowledge   10
  What do we know about dying?   14
    Where to die   14
    Communication   17
    The hospital as an organisation   18
    Dying   20
  The family   21

3 **Knowledge about Bereavement: the Data**   24

  Normal reactions to bereavement   24
  Atypical reactions to bereavement   31
  A word about the family   36
  Conclusion   37

4 **Knowledge about Dying and Bereavement:**
Interpretation   38

  The traditional approach   39
    Regression   40
    How does this help us?   42
  What about instincts: an alternative approach?   44
  Social reality   45
  Interaction and meaning   47

Social reality, dying and bereavement   49
    Cultural factors   49
    Social interaction   50
The nature of crisis   51
Conclusion   53

5   **Working with the Dying**   56

Self-knowledge   56
The context   60
The dying patient   68
    The interview   68
    The beginning   69
    The middle   70
    Ending the interview   73
    What will the patient want to discuss   77
Spiritual help   84
Using groups   85
Conclusion   87

6   **Working with the Dying Patient's Family**   90

The first encounter   90
The second interview   95
Working with the family   102

7   **Bereavement**   105

Recognising the reality of loss   110
Accepting the reality of loss and disengagement
from the deceased   113
Facing disruption and making new relationships   118
Using community resources   122

8   **Summary and Conclusions**   125

A Guide to Further Reading   133

References   137

Index   147

1
Setting the Scene

It is only when we become conscious of our own part in life, however modest, that we shall be happy. Only then will we be able to live in peace and die in peace, for only this lends meaning to life and death.

Antoine de Saint-Exupery, *Wind, Sand and Stars* (1939)

Introduction

Writing, reading and talking about death presents a particular challenge. On the one hand, death has ceased to be a topic which must be avoided or left unmentioned, as is illustrated by the burgeoning body of literature which covers the philosophical, organisational, professional and personal implications of dying, death and bereavement. On the other hand, however, it may be argued that the private and public rituals surrounding death have been gradually attenuated, and that there are few explicit guidelines for how to behave when a death occurs. There is thus an increasingly confident approach to the topic from researchers and practitioners, while at the same time personal confrontation with those who are dying or bereaved is likely to engender feelings of anxiety, confusion, uncertainty and embarrassment. A willingness and ability to talk about death with equanimity is likely to depend on the personal, social and professional significance of this event. Much of this book will be concerned with the nature of this dilemma and ways of resolving it, in relation to social work practice. It is clear that several professional groups will be involved with dying patients and their bereaved relatives. Psychiatrists, general medical practitioners, hospital staff, clergymen, home nursing personnel, are all likely to play some part in the activities surrounding death. Representatives from all these groups have made their contribution to the literature, and have explored the ways in which their professional knowledge and skills may be used to help the dying and bereaved. Researchers have looked explicitly at the organisational context of dying, communication between medical practitioners and terminally ill patients, reactions to bereavement, and a host of clinicians have commented on the 'pathological' aspects of unresolved grief and its likely causation.

My own interest in this topic has developed from both personal and professional experience. Trying to cope with the impact of two significant bereavements made me aware of the confusion and disruption attendant upon the loss of vital emotional and social relationships. My mother died in her mid-forties, following a long terminal illness. The whole family handled the problems of dying and bereavement rather badly, partly because we preferred not to recognise that my mother was terminally ill and therefore failed to respond appropriately to her growing awareness that this was the case, and partly because we made understandable but ill-informed assumptions about how to protect ourselves and others from the devastating effects of profound grief. Our family was not unusual and subsequent experience has confirmed the typical nature of our difficulties. My grandmother subsequently took over many social, emotional and practical functions previously fulfilled by my mother. Several years later my grandmother died. This bereavement differed in certain significant respects from the first; the death was sudden, my grandmother was in her seventies, and for many reasons the family was better able to cope through mutual support and shared expression of grief. At the time of these bereavements, I had only a hazy idea about how we might have been helped by social workers or medical personnel. Time has added a greater clarity in thinking and moderation in feeling.

Several years after these bereavements I took up post as a social worker in a large teaching hospital. Because of the nature of the wards to which I was attached, I found myself constantly in contact with dying patients and their families, but largely unaware of my potential role in helping them. We talked about many things but the most significant issue was scarcely mentioned. I remember a spinster dying of terminal lung cancer. She lived alone and on several occasions referred to her worry about what would happen to her budgerigar which was being cared for by neighbours. Nothing was ever said about death, but she knew that she would not be returning home to take over responsibility for her pet. Whether this lady wanted to talk about her budgie, or her life, or her death, is beside the point. The point is that I had little idea about how to respond and understood that only doctors could discuss diagnosis and prognosis with patients. I did not, therefore, allow either myself or the patient to explore what she wanted to talk about, and I have regretted it ever since.

While my unease about this whole matter was growing, two consultant surgeons with whom I was working attended a conference on care of the dying organised by the DHSS (*British Medical Journal*, 1973). They returned alarmed and amazed about their previous ignorance and thoughtlessness, and immediately conferred with me about what we could do to improve the situation. From that time, whenever a diagnosis of terminal illness was given to a patient's relatives they were asked if they would like to see the social worker, and invariably they accepted the offer. Thrown in at the deep end I learned how to help them, before and after the death of a patient. I thus have a personal and professional interest in grappling with the problems associated with dying and bereavement, and a concern that people caught up in such fundamental loss and disruption should not be left without informed guidance and support.

The issues

In any discussion about social work practice in relation to dying and bereavement, there are several issues which must be tackled. First, increasing attention has been given to the role of social workers in this context. It has been suggested that they are well placed to make an effective contribution in this area of work through their knowledge of personality development and functioning and their methods of helping people who face actual or potentially incapacitating difficulties. Some practitioners have argued that because social workers have accumulated relevant knowledge and refined appropriate practice skills, they have a professional obligation to provide a service to the dying and bereaved. I would not be writing this book, if I did not accept the validity of such an assertion. However, I do not think that the *assumption* of appropriate knowledge and skills is sufficient to convince other professional groups (particularly medical practitioners), the dying or the bereaved themselves, that social workers have an important and helpful contribution to make. Social workers who are already responding to a variety of individual, group, organisational, and political concerns also require clearly argued reasons for spending relatively scarce resources of time and emotional energy on providing a specific and well-developed service to the dying and bereaved.

Many social workers, especially those who are working in hospitals, will have contact with the terminally ill, and individuals and families who are bereaved. The devotion of a book to this subject presupposes, however, that social workers as a professional group have an important contribution to make in helping the dying and bereaved and that they should be explicitly aware of this responsibility. It also implies that social workers require some additional and specialist knowledge about these clients and appropriate techniques for working with them, which are not readily available from their established bank of information or experience. We cannot assume the validity of these two assertions given the problematic nature of social work knowledge and practice. The very flexibility of social work in recognising and attempting to deal with various areas of need, may be interpreted as being based on the suspect belief that social workers can 'be all things to all men'. Difficulties concerning the definitive characteristics of social work, or its 'inalienable element' (see *BASW*, 1977) and questions about what social workers can or should be doing in their professional capacity, are still very much matters for debate. Sheldon (1978) has argued that the knowledge base of social work is nothing more than a collection of loosely related theoretical approaches and practice models from which the eclectic social worker may pick and choose without, in most cases, the guidance of empirical investigation and evaluation. Despite Jordan's (1978) attempts to answer this criticism, I think that Sheldon has identified a continuing dilemma in knowledge and practice. The whole question of whether social work intervention is effective in helping people to lead reasonable lives which are not disrupted by incapacitating anxiety, violation of social norms and its consequences, inadequate access to power and resources as a basis for freedom of action, is still bedevilled by problems of definition, measurement and controlled research design.

In addition to all these difficulties, the conceptualisation of social work has become increasingly complex, as attempts have been made to develop a model which will incorporate the 'common core of concepts, skills, tasks and activities' (Pincus and Minahan, 1977) informing the social worker's approach to a variety of problems, across a range of individual clients and groups, at different levels of intervention. Recognition that social workers may, during the course of a day's work, move between a single parent struggling to bring up a child, to a family who cannot cope with an adolescent member's rejection of social expectations and values, to a council tenant complaining about poor housing and inadequate facilities, has prompted a critical reaction to the traditional division of social work methods into casework, group work and community work. It is clear that social workers may be using techniques from any of these approaches during contact with clients and other professional workers, and that intervention may be directed towards the manipulation of power and resources as well as manipulation of the psyche. An awareness of these factors, linked to a more realistic appreciation of the individual as functioning in a number of overlapping networks of people and material resources, has encouraged an examination of whether systems theory is relevant to developing a unitary or integrated model of social work practice. Despite some high hopes in this context, the application of systems theory to social work practice has been criticised on the grounds that it does not provide a 'theory' of practice (Forder, 1976), that its concepts have been misunderstood or applied in a rudimentary way and that in some cases, models derived from this approach have ignored or obscured the issues of power and conflict.

My purpose in making these brief observations is not to increase any sense of confusion which might already be apparent in social work circles. Indeed, lively discussion and disagreement about what constitutes appropriate knowledge, how it may be attained, and the relation between knowledge and practice may be constructive in the development of any discipline and has exercised social scientists for many years. Social work knowledge and practice is still beset by many problems concerning conceptualisation, development and selection of appropriate theoretical models, investigation and evaluation, and what Sheldon (1978) has called the great divide between the 'sloppy social worker' and the 'out of touch academic'. It is for this reason that I would recommend caution in *assuming* that social workers can and should play a central part in helping the dying and bereaved. By considering what is already known about death and bereavement, I hope to *demonstrate* that social workers are indeed well equipped to provide a service in this area of need.

The second issue which must be recognised concerns the way in which social workers might interpret the needs of the dying and bereaved. This requires information about how such people typically react to their situation and ways of understanding or 'making sense' of these reactions so that appropriate help may be offered. The way in which a social worker perceives and interprets a problem (assesses it), and the action which she subsequently decides to take in order to attain specific goals, will depend on how she understands human beings and the world in which they live and the ideological, theoretical or common-sense approach which informs such understanding. We know that social workers and clients are apt to perceive apparently the same 'problem' in different ways (Mayer and Timms, 1970) and that social workers faced with the same information may interpret it in such a way as to arrive at different assessments and different goals. As Busfield and Paddon (1977, p. x) have argued in their account of research on fertility patterns, 'data is (*sic*) not neutral, waiting to be collected and displayed according to its inherent truth and reality: any data can be understood and interpreted in a variety of different ways'. Data available to social workers, whether gleaned directly from clients or from some other source, must also be interpreted. Yet this vital step is invariably neglected in texts about social work practice. The matter of interpretation is not easy and social workers are assailed with a number of possibilities which might guide their understanding. Is it to be existentialism, psychoanalytic theory, the importance of drives or cognition, the philosophy of Zen Buddhism, or a mixture of the lot, which will inform the interpretation of data and subsequent action, and what is, or should be, the basis for choosing between them?

Any book which sets out to explore ways of helping the dying and bereaved cannot ignore the question of interpretation. This may not be popular with readers who wish to get on with the nitty gritty of what to do, but is vital if they are to be clear about *why* they have decided on a certain course of action and the most effective way of carrying it out. My own approach to the interpretation of data hinges on the notion of meaning and social reality, and will be discussed in greater detail in Chapter 4.

The third issue relates to what should be included in a book about death and social work practice. A book of this nature can provide social workers with ready access to information from a range of empirical studies and contributions from different groups of practitioners. As I was considering the inclusion of material from relevant literature and from my own experience, it became clear that a book which was only about bereavement would fail to explore the associated problems of terminally ill patients and their families. To the extent that grief reactions both before and after a death may be influenced by what happens during the course of a terminal illness, that the sense of loss associated with bereavement may also be experienced by those who are dying, and that the whole family will be affected by the terminal illness of one of its members, it seemed imperative to write about dying as well as bereavement. Thus, while this book is about reactions to bereavement, the experience and expression of grief, and the process of mourning, it is also about dying, and the meaning of loss for all those individuals and groups who will feel its impact and respond in similar ways.

Fourth, it must be acknowledged that talking about death and working with the dying and bereaved faces the practitioner with fundamental questions about life, death and meaning. While the amount of literature on this subject indicates a growing willingness to discuss the matter, confronting those who are dying or bereaved is likely to impose additional strains. Ginsberg (1977) has remarked that facing the reality of death not only touches upon personal fears and anxieties, but also presents social workers with difficulties which cannot be ameliorated in the usual way through helping people to either modify the problem or adapt more successfully to the demands of social interaction and their own and other's expectations. How does one change the problem when a vital participant and resource is removed from the scene? How does one adapt to a situation when no amount of professional intervention can help in attaining the goal of reunion with the lost object? Social workers are also likely to be co-operating with other professional groups and must take into account what death means to them. Kübler-Ross (1970) comments wryly that when she wanted to interview a terminally ill patient, 'it suddenly seemed that there were no dying patients in this huge hospital'. The loss of power and ability to exercise control which is experienced by doctors and nurses caring for terminally ill patients has also been discussed by Benoliel (1974), who suggests that the expression of grief by medical personnel is inhibited by the structural conditions in which they work. Social workers need to understand and respond appropriately to the feelings of those around them. Pincus and Minahan's (1977) reference to the significance of an action system also emphasises that skills are required as much in working with other professional groups as in providing a service to clients.

There are several ways of approaching the complicated

topic of dying and bereavement. We could consider the implications of death for widows, widowers, children who have
lost a parent, parents who have lost children, and families
who have suffered a bereavement. The stresses involved for
medical personnel and families who are caring for handicapped
and terminally ill children have also been given considerable
attention. I have decided to focus on dying and bereavement
from the perspective of adults and their families. Much of the
following discussion will be relevant to children who are
terminally ill or who face bereavement, and many of the
practice issues will be common to all individuals and groups
who experience actual or impending loss. This book can only
be a guide to practice in so far as it sensitises the reader to
some of the issues mentioned above and provides some concepts and tools for making them emotionally, cognitively and
practically manageable.

It should be noted that for practical reasons, social workers
will be referred to in the feminine gender throughout the
following chapters, while clients and others will be referred
to in the masculine gender.

2
Knowledge about Dying: the Data

I stood once with three peasants in the presence of their dead mother. Sorrow filled the room. For a second time, the umbilical cord had been cut. For a second time the knot had been loosed, the knot that bound one generation to another.

Antoine de Saint-Exupery, *Wind, Sand and Stars* (1939)

A few words about knowledge

The whole question of what constitutes knowledge and how we can develop it is complex, and has posed a central problem in the social sciences in relation to theory and methods of social investigation. Given that social work texts frequently mention knowledge, it is perhaps surprising that we appear to take for granted both what we mean by this term and how we think we come by such knowledge. References are commonly made to data, information, beliefs, values, knowledge-base, self-knowledge and procedures of diagnosis, assessment and evaluation, as if it is self-evident that everyone understands what is being discussed. I have already referred to knowledge and practice in the preceding chapter, and before going any further it is important to explain exactly what I mean.

Timms and Timms (1977) are among the few writers on social work who have considered it important to give some attention to the problem of knowledge. They suggest that knowledge is what we believe to be the case on the basis of information or evidence at our disposal. The most important question for social work involves what is considered to be acceptable evidence. Timms and Timms go on to outline three different kinds of knowledge: first, there is knowledge that something is, in fact, the case, which involves empirical evidence about typical behaviour in certain situations, or the ability to generalise about the relationship between variables. The second is what they call 'knowledge by acquaintance', which seems to parallel the accumulation of experience through continued contact with a client group, a neighbourhood, an agency and so on. Third, is knowledge about how to do something (as distinct from being able to do it), which Timms and Timms refer to as 'know-how'.

A consideration of knowledge is an important issue for social work generally and for any discussion about how best to help the dying and bereaved. As Leonard (1975) correctly points out, social workers are not only faced with many and conflicting explanations of human behaviour, but also with disagreements about what constitutes acceptable evidence and appropriate methods for collecting it. This difficulty is likely to have played some part in the tendency of social workers to avoid any reference to general statements about behaviour and to rely on their subjective understanding of individual feelings or events in both assessing and responding to problems and, in association with this, to translate information or ideas which may be cognitively grasped, into expressions of feeling. How often, for example, do social workers discuss their views or decisions in terms of what they feel, rather than what they think? Timms and Timms conclude that, 'we are convinced that in relation to knowledge social workers use a very over-simplified version of feeling' (1977, p. 119). Now, the difficulties associated with what constitutes knowledge and evidence are well recognised by writers in the social sciences. Sociologists have long struggled with the question of how to understand social phenomena and the particular methods of investigation which such an undertaking requires. The problem is not new, but what is noteworthy in this context is social workers' apparent unwillingness to recognise and tackle it. Sheldon (1978) has asserted that until social workers come to grips with the problems of knowledge and research, the divide between theory and practice, or the 'out-of-touch academic' and the 'sloppy social worker', will not be resolved.

I have made this short excursion into a consideration of knowledge for two major reasons. First, Jordan has commented in his introduction to Lonsdale, Elfer and Ballard (1979) that 'all three authors emphasise that humility and respect are more valued qualities in such work than flashy therapeutic skills', and that the role of 'comforter is as relevant as ever'. I would agree entirely with the sentiment which he expresses, but all the humility, respect and comforting in the world is of little consequence if we do not know why it is important and how it can help someone cope with the problems of everyday life. The 'why' of the matter involves knowledge about the nature of the problem itself and what to do about it. Second, my reference to knowledge includes both what we know to be the case, that is evidence about how people react to dying and bereavement, what is 'normal' and what is 'abnormal' in the sense of enabling people to function adequately in their families, at work, in society, and how we interpret or make sense of this evidence: that is, description and explanation respectively. I have distinguished this knowledge from practice because of the relation which I consider to exist between them. If we know how the dying and bereaved typically respond to their situation and understand why this is the case, then we are likely to develop a pretty good idea about how to help them. Our means of helping – methods, techniques, strategies of intervention – whatever we wish to call them, may then be evaluated and yield more knowledge about either their general effectiveness in helping clients with certain typically occurring problems, or in specific cases enabling client and social worker to attain the goal(s) which they have agreed. Knowing how to do something can thus become knowledge in the sense suggested by Timms and Timms (1977). Although I have suggested that knowledge, including description and understanding, comes first in this sequence of events, it may of course happen that social workers cannot ask a distressed client to wait while they run off and do the odd bit of research, read the relevant book or acquire the necessary knowledge.

However, if knowledge has already been accumulated by researchers and practitioners, it is as much the social worker's responsibility to attempt to grasp it as it is to respond to a client's distress, no matter how humble, respectful and comforting the worker is able to be. It is for this reason that part of this book will be concerned with knowledge, that is with description and understanding. To launch straight into a guide to practice without giving attention to knowledge about dying and bereavement would show a lack of respect for social workers and the people whom we are seeking to help. Where social workers are co-operating with other professional colleagues, as they will often be doing, there is likely to be some discussion about what should be done, who is to do it, and how it should be accomplished. If social workers are to have an informed and acceptable part in such exchanges, their contribution must be based on knowledge.

Medical colleagues are likely to react with impatience when confronted by social workers wishing to take a certain course of action, whose only justification for their view is that it is subjectively 'self-evident' or they 'feel' that this should be so. In a similar way it is difficult to justify to the press or the agency that informed action was taken in returning a child to the care of natural parents, or removing a child from their care, if we cannot refer to our knowledge about risk factors in family functioning or child development. If knowledge cannot be demonstrated to have a significant part in decision-making, then social workers have little defence against the accusation that decisions are ill-informed or based mainly on their feelings, intuition, personal values, or even panic reactions.

The importance of self-knowledge in social work, specifically with regard to working with the dying and bereaved, will be considered in the practice section of this book. This is because, while self-knowledge is vital to the social work endeavour and while social workers may develop a stock of knowledge concerning how they typically feel about and respond to certain kinds of clients or situations, knowing oneself (as a social worker) both grows out of practice and is an input to practice in a continuing process of reflection and evaluation.

This chapter is concerned with one aspect of knowledge — that is, what we know about the dying and bereaved from evidence about their behaviour, and the behaviour of those around them. Such evidence is usually comprised of what they say and observations about how they act. Chapter 4 will consider the second aspect of knowledge which I have noted — that is, how we can understand and make sense of the available data about dying and bereavement.

What do we know about dying?

Where to die?

In 1960, Hughes noted that more than half of the deaths in Britain occurred out of hospital. Cartwright *et al.* (1973) comment that the percentage of people dying in hospital has increased over time, and that in 1969 over half the recorded deaths took place in hospital. The proportion of people dying at home has also decreased from 49 per cent in 1954 to 39 per cent in 1969. Strauss and Glaser (1975) suggest that less than one-third of all deaths in the USA take place outside a hospital or institutional setting. Cartwright *et al.* suggest various reasons for this trend, including increased mobility, greater numbers of women working ouside the home, and smaller nuclear families which may be separated both geographically and in terms of values and life-style from their extended kinship network. Even given that the extended family may continue to function as an important source of social and emotional support, it may still be increasingly difficult for relatives to provide home care for a terminally ill patient. On the basis of information from various studies, Hinton (1967, p. 69) concludes that, 'although a small proportion are struck down suddenly and a small proportion have months of being seriously ill before they die, the majority will have a terminal period requiring special care lasting a few days or weeks and not usually exceeding three months'.

Since the question of whether or not terminally ill patients can be cared for at home is likely to be considered by doctors, the patient, and his family, it is important to assess what is known about the advantages and disadvantages of returning home from hospital.

Cartwright *et al.* collected information about the last year of life of 785 randomly selected people, who died in twelve areas of England and Wales during certain periods in 1968 and 1969. Wherever possible interviews were conducted with the person who had notified the registrar of a death. 91 per cent of the deceased population had spent some time at home during their last year of life, and 80 per cent were at home for most of the time. Approximately 48 per cent died in their own or somebody else's home. Informants reported several symptoms which either they, or the patient, found distressing in the twelve months preceding death. These were pain (66 per cent), sleeplessness (49 per cent), loss of appetite (48 per cent) and trouble with breathing (45 per cent), as well as others less frequently mentioned. Just over two-thirds had one or more symptoms which informants reported as being distressing.

Nearly a third of the deceased had needed some help with personal care for at least a year prior to death, and just over one-fifth had needed attention for a month or longer. Over half the people spending sometime at home during their last year of life had had ten or more consultations with their general practitioner, and yet it was reported that no help had been sought from this source for a quarter of the symptoms experienced by patients. 29 per cent of the symptoms about which no advice had been asked, were described as 'very distressing'. Cartwright *et al.* find it disturbing that this was the case and conclude:

> failure to recognise needs for community services which can help relatives and friends in the care of patients at home suggests that general practitioners do not give as much support as they might to caring relatives, nor do the doctors always seem to appreciate the amount of care that relatives and friends provide, or the extent and full nature of patients' needs in the last year of their lives (p. 103).

Cartwright *et al.* also highlight the problems experienced by those who cared for terminally ill patients at home. Social isolation, loss of social contacts, tiredness, emotional stress and health problems were frequently mentioned.

Aitken-Swan (1959) followed up relatives of 200 patients who had died of cancer but who had been nursed for a period at home. In 62 per cent of cases, relatives reported that patients had wished to stay at home or that they had wanted to care for them at home. In summary, 75 per cent of respondents considered that terminal care had been adequate, 14 per cent of patients had finally been admitted to hospital or a terminal-care institution while in 15 per cent of cases, despite requests for this, admission had not been arranged. 77 per cent of respondents were satisfied with the patients' medical care at home, but in 20 per cent of cases patients were reported to have suffered severe and unrelieved pain. A third of the people interviewed referred to the 'severe strain' of caring for patients at home and identified heavy lifting, washing, other illness in the house, sitting up during the night, and lack of social support, as being significant reasons for this. Corroboration for some of these findings is provided by Parkes (1977) in his follow-up study of the spouses of patients who had been cared for at St Christopher's Hospice in London, for at least some period during their terminal illness. Parkes suggests that if patients are to receive adequate care at home, their symptoms must be amenable to relief, the family must be able to cope, and the local community health services must be well informed and prepared to help. Less than a third of patients who had been at home during their terminal illness met these conditions for adequate care. The major reasons for failure of home care and the associated distress of patients and family were first, the unwillingness of general practitioners to prescribe adequate pain-relieving drugs, and second, poor communication with doctors so that families did not always ask for or receive appropriate help.

Evidence would suggest that although some patients and their families may wish to spend the terminal period together at home, this is likely to present problems regarding adequate pain control, the provision of community medical resources, and practical, emotional, and social stresses for the patient and family.

Communication

There is now accumulating evidence from empirical studies to confirm the widely suspected fact that communication between doctors and patients and their families, is often extremely poor. Patients and relatives have been found to be dissatisfied with information given, often because it was insufficient, they did not understand the terminology, they were confused, and they felt too diffident to seek clarification. Robinson (1973) has reviewed some of the literature on this topic, and comments that many studies are characterised by an emphasis on how doctors can conveniently and efficiently get information over to patients, and not by a concern about facilitating the patient's satisfaction with communication and understanding of his situation. Patients and relatives are also influenced by worries about taking up the valuable time of medical personnel in order to seek information (Stacey *et al.*, 1970). Where relatives or patients are working class, difficulties relating to diffidence, social distance, different forms of verbal expression, and doctors' expectations of their ability to understand information, have also been shown to be significant in influencing effective communication.

Given the apparent difficulties in communication already noted, it would seem likely that the exchange of information about terminal illness would be even more problematic. Studies have shown that the views of medical personnel are consistently against giving information to terminally ill patients regarding the diagnosis and prognosis of their condition. If terminally ill patients either do not suspect that they are dying or do not want to know the diagnosis and/or prognosis, such a position could arguably be in the best interests of everyone concerned. However, Hinton (1967) found that at least 49 per cent of the patients in a general hospital 'were neither ignorant nor evasive of the fact that their illness might be fatal', and 'half of those people dying in hospital, even at the first interview, took the opportunity to talk frankly and spoke of the possibility or certainty that they were to die soon' (p. 97). Other studies have shown that at least half the patients with terminal illness were aware of the diagnosis, and the great majority of these were also aware that they were likely to die in the foreseeable future. Kübler-Ross (1970) and Saunders (1959 and 1974), from long experience of working with the terminally ill, suggest that the proportion of those who know that they are dying is much higher than 50 per cent.

McIntosh (1977), on the basis of observing doctors and patients and talking to both groups, asserted that while doctors thought that some patients should be told about their condition and its likely outcome, they did not know which patients would be able to cope with the information and therefore told no one. He also observed that while doctors said they responded to individual patients in relation to their particular enquiries, they in fact gave typically constructed responses to what they perceived as general types of communication.

Empirical investigation thus shows that patients' needs for information and the opportunity to talk about death, are not individually assessed, that patients are likely to be socially and emotionally isolated with their unexpressed fears and anxieties about the future, and that relatives warned not to tell patients about their condition are confused and distressed by their powerlessness and the conspiracy of silence in which they are caught. Saunders (1973) notes the reply of a man who knew he was dying to her question about what he looked for in those around him. He said, 'for someone to look as if they were trying to understand me'. She comments, 'he did not ask for success, he asked for the effort of trying' (p. 30).

The hospital as an organisation

Much has been written about the organisational characteristics of hospital and other forms of institutional care. In this context questions concerning hierarchical conflicts, power, resource allocation and professional issues have been identified as being particularly relevant. Sudnow (1967) and Strauss and Glaser (1975) have pointed to the emphasis on technical competence and efficiency in hospital organisation and service delivery, which also govern methods of dealing with terminally ill patients and their families. Cartwright *et al.* (1973) noted that between a quarter and three-tenths of hospital bed-days annually are taken up by patients who will be dead within a year, and that this will account for something like 15 per cent of expenditure on health and welfare services. They suggest, however, that general hospitals are not organised and the staff are not trained to offer effective care to the dying patient and his family, and that with careful assessment it would be possible for such patients to have a much more positive experience in their last year of life if cared for in the community.

There is little evidence that social workers are seen as significant members of the hospital team when it comes to caring for terminally ill patients and their families, except in relatively few special units and hospices for the dying. It has been recognised that there are difficulties with regard to professional status, communication, different priorities and approaches to decision-making, in interaction between doctors and social workers. When I suggested that social workers should be viewed as members of the health care team rather than as a fringe luxury (Smith, 1973) my proposition was greeted with hostility by some doctors. At the same time, research findings have indicated that hospital docotrs do not generally respond to the individual needs of terminally ill patients or their families, and at least some members of the medical profession have recognised inadequacies in training for an awareness of the social and emotional implications of illness (see for example, Jeffreys, 1975; Balint, 1964).

Further evidence concerning the minimal use of social workers in hospitals is provided by two studies on childless couples and their experience of infertility investigations. Smith (1980) found that although couples reported a high degree of anxiety, distress, and communication problems during infertility investigations, only seven out of eighty-six respondents recalled having been told that they could see a medical social worker. The great majority of those who had not been told said that they would have liked to make use of this service had they known a social worker was available. Burnage (1976, p. 24) investigating the same topic notes, 'the medical social worker has not so far been mentioned, mainly because I never met anyone who had seen her, or been referred to her'.

It would thus appear that, while we know certain aspects of hospital organisation and the training and practice of medical practitioners are not designed to facilitate a recognition of patients' social and emotional problems or to respond to these, social work services are not generally used to help either patients or their families in this context.

Dying

Kübler-Ross (1970) has identified five stages through which a patient is likely to pass as he moves towards death, although it should be recognised that patients may move between these at various times. Her observations are based on lengthy experience of working with terminally ill patients and her findings are generally corroborated by Hinton (1967) and Saunders (1959 and 1974). First, on coming to know that they are dying, patients react with denial, and this response may be repeated at various times until their death. Second, the patient is likely to be frustrated and angry. Such anger will be expressed towards a number of people, but if it is directed at members of the family a situation may arise where 'they then either respond with grief and tears, guilt or shame, or avoid future visits, which only increases the patient's discomfort and anger' (Kübler-Ross, p. 45). Third, the patient is likely to bargain, with God, with doctors, with anyone who may be able to help them postpone the inevitable. Fourth, when anger and bargaining have clearly not achieved the desired result, depression is likely to follow. Kübler-Ross distinguishes between the reactive depression of this stage which is a response to loss of freedom, the ability to function normally, habitual roles, and preparatory depression when a patient begins to withdraw from social interaction in the acknowledgement of approaching death. Fifth, and not all patients reach this stage, is acceptance. The patient is ready to detach himself from meaningful relationships and to accept the finality of death. At this stage death is often seen as a relief by people who have been ill for some time, while it is difficult for family and friends to understand that a patient may be ready to give up the fight for life.

Hinton (1963 and 1967) has commented on the anxiety suffered by terminally ill patients and he identifies fear of pain as playing a significant part in this. It is important to recognise, however, that pain may be a complex combination of physical pain and psychological distress and that steps taken to alleviate the latter may have repercussions in fewer complaints about the former. Anxiety may also be generated by the emotional and social separation of a patient from family and friends. The fear of separation and painful procedures has also been identified in children with serious illness. Physical separation through hospitalisation causes anxiety and depression in some patients, but the commonly observed emotional withdrawal or avoidance by family and friends has also been noted as influencing the degree of distress experienced by those who are dying.

Evidence from researchers and practitioners thus alerts us to the typical responses of dying patients, the realistic basis for their anxieties, and the apparent difficulties experienced by professional staff, family and friends, in knowing how to react to terminally ill people.

The family

There has been relatively little empirical investigation specifically concerning the problems and reactions of the dying patient's family, and much of what has been done has focused on terminally ill children. It is clear however, from the consistent observations of practitioners and researchers concerned with dying patients, that families with terminally ill members face a number of difficulties. First, there is the problem of communicaiton. While relatives are usually aware of the diagnosis and prognosis, patients are not, and there is some evidence to suggest that relatives are encouraged by medical staff to withhold such information from patients (Cartwright *et al.*, 1973). At any rate, family members are in possession of important information and are likely to be uncertain about how to handle it. We have seen above, that relatives may react by emotional and social withdrawal from the patient. Orcutt (1977) notes that in his current research with high risk and dying patients, one of the most frequently observed responses was 'closure of communication'. Where patients knew their diagnosis and family members understood the full implications of diagnosis and prognosis, a common pattern emerged where each tried to protect the other from acknowledging the situation and expressing their feelings. He remarks, 'if the patient seems depressed, withdrawn, or silent or expresses his grief in tears, this usually leads the family and others to avoid these feelings rather than give him the opportunity to share his grief' (Orcutt, 1977, p. 26). There is also evidence to suggest that parents experience difficulty in sharing and acknowledging their children's anxiety about the outcome of their illness and in telling children that a family member is terminally ill or has died.

Kübler-Ross (1970) has observed the difficulties of families in coping with the dying patient's anger, and the mutual distress and feelings of rejection which may lead to confusion and avoidance. Lack of understanding of a patient's preparatory depression and readiness to die, and the social and emotional withdrawal which may accompany this, is likely to leave family members feeling rejected, shut out, or angry with the patient for 'giving up' and abdicating his responsibilities to those around him.

In addition to the emotional and social difficulties of communicating and interacting with dying patients, family members have many practical problems with which to contend. Kaplan *et al.* (1973, p. 62) have asserted that 'the family with a leukemic child is also suddenly confronted with major alterations in its circumstances that threaten cherished hopes and values for all its members and involve drastic alterations in their life-style'. The research of Cohen *et al.* (1977) has identified particular problems for families during the terminal illness, and following the death of a mother. Their data indicate that fewer difficulties in post-death restabilisation were experienced by families classified as having open and free internal communication, and flexibility in the assignment of role expectations. However, those families where the mother had died had poorer ratings on communication patterns than others. Even families with good communication reported greater difficulties in managing household tasks following the death of a mother, and family members were also more likely to become ill during the terminal phase if it was the mother who was dying. If mothers serve to function as significant facilitators of family communication and affective exchanges, their absence from interaction will have implications for the family's ability to provide these resources and to reorganise role expectations and communication patterns effectively (Vollman *et al.* 1971; Williams *et al.*, 1972).

We know a great deal about the organisational and professional constraints which influence the quality of care for those who are dying at home or in hospital, about the feelings and responses of dying patients, and about the reactions and problems of family members whether these are related to their interaction with those who are terminally ill or the tension of internal readjustment and communication. But we might be allowed a moment's surprise about the dearth of evidence concerning the social worker's actual or potential contribution in this context; for it is apparent that in Britain, although less so in the USA, social work has not generally played a significant part in providing care for the dying patient and his family.

3
Knowledge about Bereavement: the Data

I did not know what to say to him. I felt awkward and blundering. I did not know how I could reach him, where I could overtake him and go hand in hand with him once more. It is such a secret place, the land of tears.

Antoine de Saint-Exupery, *The Little Prince* (1945)

Investigators interested in bereavement have applied themselves to a number of questions. They have been variously concerned with sociological description and explanation, clinical features of 'normal' and 'abnormal' reactions, programmes for prevention, the relation between bereavement and other kinds of loss, and different cultural forms of mourning. In order to disentangle the complex range of available information, it is useful to consider research findings under several headings.

Normal reactions to bereavement

In the following discussion, the term grief should be understood to refer to subjective responses to bereavement and their outward expression, while mourning denotes the process of feeling and expressing grief and the cultural and institutional forms which this may take. In so far as any bereavement reaction is likely to involve distress and some impairment of normal functioning, and to have recognisable characteristics and duration, it has been suggested that it should be viewed as a 'disease' or 'mental disorder' (Parkes, 1965; Engel, 1961). It is argued that such a position would challenge medical researchers and practitioners to take a serious interest in the nature and process of grief reactions.

A great deal of evidence is already available about the outcome of bereavement. On the basis of his observations of 101 bereaved individuals, Lindemann (1944) identified a recognisable pattern of reactions, and explored the deviations from this which may characterise what he called 'morbid' or abnormal grief. In summary, he suggested that typical grief reactions can be described in terms of first, somatic (physical) distress; second, preoccupation with thoughts and an image of the deceased; third, guilt feelings; fourth, hostile reactions and irritability towards a variety of people including the deceased; fifth, restlessness and hyperactivity without any organised pattern of conduct or the ability to establish and achieve goals. Marris (1958) interviewed seventy-two widows living in London, aged between 25 and 56 years old, whose husbands had died on average two years and two months before the research was carried out. Common reactions to bereavement which were identified by the widows included difficulty in sleeping (fifty-seven), deterioration in health (thirty-one), loss of contact with reality (forty-seven), sense of dead husband's presence (thirty-six), apathy (forty-four), withdrawal from social interaction (twenty-seven), hostility and irritability (twenty-five). Only eight widows specifically mentioned having experienced feelings of guilt. Gorer (1965) identified similar reactions to bereavement from detailed interviews with eighty people who had suffered the death of various close relatives, although he suggests that the expression of guilt and anger were less pronounced in his research findings. Marris argues from his evidence that widows are faced with a number of conflicts relating to their loss. They must give up believing that their loss is not real, while at the same time this reality is avoided because of the pain and despair which it entails. Their need for companionship and understanding is great, but because this threatens their sense of independence and intrudes upon maintaining respect for relationships with their dead husbands, they tend to respond with hostility and irritability to those who offer consolation. The widow's inability to relate to others, financial difficulties, and constraints imposed by child rearing, may lead to increasing social isolation.

Parkes (1972) has carried out extensive empirical investigations of bereavement and explores both typical and atypical reactions to loss, particularly among relatively young widows. He suggests that bereavement constitutes a loss of security which is perceived as threatening and which produces a state of stress and alarm. Initially, the bereaved may comprehend their loss at one level while denying its reality at another, and their anxiety may lead to searching aimed at recovering the lost object. Parkes characterises this stage by alarm, tension, restlessness, preoccupation with thoughts about and the image of the dead person, loss of interest in goal achievement and personal appearance, calling for the lost person, and a focus of attention on places where the lost person is likely to be found. He thus accounts for observations of restlessness, activity, and tension, in terms of specific attempts to locate the lost person, and suggests that reports concerning seeing, hearing, talking to, and dreaming about the dead individual are reflections of this attempt at searching and finding. Other researchers have noted that the bereaved frequently experience a sense of the presence of their dead relatives, and find themselves acting towards them as if the loss had not occurred. General irritability and anger were also identified during the early stage of mourning. With the decrease in searching (and finding) activity, and an increasing recognition of the reality of loss, the bereaved typically experience a period where feelings of aimlessness, disorganisation and despair predominate. Habitual activities and roles previously defined by reference to the lost person, become redundant and inappropriate. Activity is disorganised and meaningless until the development of new patterns of interaction and new goals which do not depend on reciprocal action from the dead person for their fulfilment. Gradually the bereaved pick up their old social contacts, develop new relationships, and define new goals whether in terms of going out to work, bringing up their children, seeking out new activities, carrying on some interest of the dead person, and by doing so begin to establish a modified identity and purpose.

Battin *et al.* (1977) report on the reactions of fifty-eight families, three months, six months and three to five years after bereavement. Although some diminution of the sample occurred over the research period, the typically expected responses were identified. During the first three months following bereavement, respondents reported feelings of worthlessness, emptiness, wishing to believe the deceased was still alive and a preoccupation with memories about the dead person. Other frequently expressed reactions were fear of death or going mad, hopelessness, anxiety, depression, suspiciousness, anger, irritability and concern about new responsibilities. As in other studies, difficulty in sleeping, tiredness and tension were often noted as being problems for the bereaved. When this group was followed up six months after their bereavement, most of the distressing responses to loss had diminished and continued to do so until the last contact three to five years later. Battin *et al.* note that at the sixth-month follow-up, greater numbers of the bereaved were feeling needed by others, relatively contented, and more hopeful about the future than during the initial contact. The majority of respondents reported having this positive outlook by the last phase of the research. Guilt feelings were observed less frequently than the authors expected, and diminished rapidly during the first six months of bereavement.

Clayton *et al.* (1968) attempted to identify major reactions to bereavement amongst the many responses noted by other researchers. Forty bereaved individuals were interviewed nearly a month after their loss, and rather fewer of the original sample were subsequently seen between one and four months after the death. The authors conclude that only three symptoms were consistently reported by over half the respondents. These were depressed mood, sleep disturbance and crying. Although difficulty in concentrating, loss of interest in outside events, and anorexia or weight loss were also frequently noted, they occurred in less than half the sample. At the second series of interviews, 81 per cent of the bereaved said that they had improved, and Clayton *et al.* comment that, 'it is clear that in an unselected population bereavement is a relatively mild reaction for most subjects' (p. 177). They also remark that psychiatrists are generally unlikely to be working with people who suffer normal grief reactions, since 98 per cent of their respondents reported that they had improved without seeking psychiatric help.

Additional empirical data also suggest that the recently bereaved consult their doctors about psychological symptoms more frequently than was their practice before bereavement. When compared with control subjects in the general population an increased incidence of consultation was also found for the bereaved group. While this appears to be the case for relatively young bereaved people, those aged 65 and over do not appear to show the same increased consultation rate with regard to psychological difficulties. However, all age groups of the bereaved appear to experience a greater number of physical complaints which are brought to the attention of their doctors, than was the case before their bereavement. In association with this, there is evidence that the bereaved (particularly widows and widowers) suffer increased mortality when compared to the expected incidence for non-bereaved members of the general population. As Parkes (1972) points out, these statistical findings do not explain the reasons for a relatively high incidence of mortality among the bereaved, and there are a number of possible interpretations both of these data and of those concerning the higher frequency of medical consultations for psychological and physical symptoms. However, such information does point to the increased vulnerability of the bereaved in relation to emotional and physical health.

Some studies have attempted to discover whether there is any difference between grief reactions of those who have had some prior warning about an impending death, for example in the case of a relatively long terminal illness, and those who have experienced a sudden and unexpected death. Available evidence on this matter appears to be inconsistent. Clayton *et al.* (1968) found that the only difference reaching statistical significance, was with regard to symptoms of anorexia or weight loss experienced by those whose relatives had suffered relatively short terminal illnesses. They suggest that this may be due to the disruption of normal routines and a fairly short, intensive period of anxiety. Schwab *et al.* (1975) reported that extended terminal illnessess (longer than one year) were significantly associated with a higher percentage of intense grief reactions, as compared with illnesses of less than a years duration or deaths which were not preceded by illness. Bornstein *et al.* (1973), however, found no evidence of an association between sudden bereavement and extreme or long-standing grief reactions. In a carefully conducted study, Parkes (1975) compared the responses of relatively young widows and widowers (under 45 year old) in relation to the duration of their spouses' terminal illness and their forewarning of imminent death. Those who said that they had less than two weeks' warning that their spouses' illness was likely to be fatal or less than three days' notice of imminent death (24 respondents) were termed the 'short preparation group', while the 'long preparation group' (46 respondents) had experienced a longer period with the knowledge that their spouses were terminally ill. At the first interview, three weeks after bereavement, the 'long preparation group' were generally less confused, more able to accept the reality of their loss, and markedly less likely to express feelings of guilt and anger, than the 'short preparation group'. A year later, members of the 'long preparation group' were significantly more likely to have achieved a 'good' outcome, than were those in the other group. This difference was maintained at follow-up two to four years later. In comparing his own results with those of Bornstein *et al.*, Parkes concludes that the difference in their findings is likely to be attributable to the relatively elderly sample in the former's study. Nearly half of Bornstein *et al.*'s respondents were over 60 years old, and there is evidence to suggest that the elderly bereaved experience a less severe emotional reaction to loss than the relatively young.

Parkes (1975) suggests, therefore, that a severe and prolonged reaction to bereavement is more likely to occur when a death is perceived as being both sudden and untimely. Schiff (1977), writing about the death of her 10-year-old son, considers that parents facing the death of a child have particularly severe problems of adjustment given what is perceived to be an untimely, unnatural and unjust loss. Those who have some warning that a terminal illness will prove fatal, are provided with the opportunity to do all they can

for the dying person and to avoid guilt which may be associated with poor communication, strained relationships, and
inappropriate behaviour prior to their bereavement. They will
also have time to anticipate changes in social interaction and
role performance, and may even have begun to accommodate
these if the terminal illness has been of long duration. Some
support for Parkes's findings is provided by Cartwright *et al.*
(1973).

There has been a good deal of interest in how far people
are able to grieve and come to terms with loss, before a significant other has actually died. Gerber (1974) suggests that
relatives of a dying patient may be able to use the terminal
phase to plan for the time when they will be bereaved. He
asserts that 'anticipatory bereavement can be looked upon as
a period of socialisation into the bereaved role'. The implica-
tion of such a view is that grief reactions following a death
are likely to be less severe than in those cases where there is
little or no opportunity for anticipating and practising a new
role in advance of actual bereavement. It may well be the
case that terminal illness necessitates adjustments in role fulfilment and that some practical issues may have been tackled
before bereavement. However, there are two important points
which should be remembered. First, when someone is dying
the activities of family members are likely to revolve around
hospital visits or caring for the patient at home. Conversation,
making arrangements, organising time, will be focused on the
terminally ill person. Thus, when death occurs, the impact of
loss and feelings of disorganisation and meaninglessness are
likely to be acutely experienced even though there may have
been a period of 'anticipatory bereavement'. Second, if dying
family members are hospitalised it becomes gradually taken
for granted that they are no longer physically present in the
domestic context. In some cases it may therefore be possible
for the bereaved to avoid the reality of loss through continuing the assumption that the deceased person is 'somewhere
else'. Thus, while actual bereavement may lead to disorganisation contingent upon the disruption of daily routines, hospital
visits, and so on, at the same time it may be difficult to grasp
the reality of death when this occurs following a period of
hospital care.

Attempts to establish the nature of grief reactions in relation to anticipation of bereavement, have neglected to consider the *quality* of interaction between those who are dying and those who will suffer the loss. Although difficult to measure, mutually rewarding communication and the maintenance of supportive relationships during a terminal illness would be more likely to facilitate a 'good' outcome following bereavement. Given the evidence which is available, it seems reasonable to suggest that help given during a terminal illness may not only improve the immediate situation for the dying patient and close relatives, but may have long-term benefits through facilitating a less severe response to bereavement.

Apart from the question of the nature of grief reactions, as observed by clinical practitioners and reported by the bereaved, it is useful to have some idea of the expected time scale for recovery in normal bereavement. Parkes (1965a) notes that the features of acute grief would normally begin to moderate in intensity during the first six weeks following bereavement, and to be minimal by six months. Empirical evidence from follow-up studies also indicates that affective and behavioural responses can be expected to have significantly changed towards normal patterns by six months after a bereavement. While we would thus anticipate the moderation of grief reactions during the first six months, it should be noted that some problems, for example financial and child-rearing difficulties, isolation and loneliness, may increase as time passes. It should also be recognised that important anniversaries, family gatherings, and personally upsetting events may bring about renewed pangs of grief.

Atypical reactions to bereavement

By atypical reactions to bereavement, I mean that pattern of responses which is not amenable to the expected process of moderation and abatement, and which significantly interferes with personal and social functioning to the extent that professional help may be sought by the bereaved. Such reactions have variously been referred to as pathological, complicated, or morbid by other writers on the subject. On the basis of two studies, Parkes (1964; 1965a; 1965b) suggests that there is an association between admission for psychiatric treatment and the onset of presenting symptoms within six months of a major bereavement. The number of bereaved psychiatric patients was greater than would have been expected if the association had only occurred by chance. Other authors have also noted the apparent relationship between current losses or threats of loss and the onset of psychiatric disorders.

Anyone concerned with helping the bereaved should be aware of the possibility that recovery may not proceed normally. They should also be able to identify signs of atypical grief reactions, and so far as present knowledge allows, be sensitive to factors which may increase the vulnerability of the bereaved in relation to coping successfully with their loss. Parkes asserts that the most common single diagnosis among psychiatric patients who had been bereaved, was reactive or neurotic depression. In an attempt to define the characteristics of atypical grief reactions, Parkes used Marris's (1958) study as a baseline for comparison. He concluded that psychiatric patients who were suffering from atypical grief were significantly more likely to express feelings of guilt and self-blame, and to have greater difficulty accepting their loss, than were the unselected sample described in Marris's study. Other atypical features shown by psychiatric patients were abnormal duration of grief, unusually intense grief, delayed reaction to bereavement, hypochondriacal symptoms comparable to those suffered by the deceased, and panic attacks. It would thus appear from Parkes's analysis that while atypical grief reactions may be similar in kind to normal patterns of grief, they are characterised by some degree of exaggeration or distortion which incapacitates the individual and suggests the need for psychiatric help.

Parkes (1965b) defines several categories of atypical grief. These are first, inhibited grief, where expected reactions to bereavement are either absent or expressed in distorted ways. Second, chronic grief, where usual reactions are apparent but recovery does not appear to take a normal time-limited course. Third, delayed grief, where recognising the reality of loss and expressing grief is postponed and experienced with particular severity at a later date. Lindemann

(1944) suggests that 'the most striking and most frequent' of atypical grief reactions is a delay or postponement in recognising and expressing grief. During the period of postponement Lindemann asserts that the individual may be observed to be overactive, to acquire symptoms associated with the illness of the deceased, to develop a psychosomatic disease, to withdraw from family and friends, to be hostile to others, to respond in a 'wooden' or formal manner, to engage in self-punitive behaviour. Such reactions may lead to 'a straight agitated depression with tension, agitation, insomnia, feelings of worthlessness, bitter self-accusation and obvious need for punishment' (Lindemann, 1944, p. 146). Volkan (1975) also suggests that the 'pathological mourner' may be identified by an attitude of intellectual acknowledgement of loss accompanied by emotional denial of this reality six months or more after bereavement. This atypical form of grief reaction similar to that of delay or postponement, is seen in the bereaved individual who 'becomes fixated in the initial reactions to death and is caught in the struggle of loss and restitution without coming to resolution' (Volkan, 1975, p. 335). Volkan describes a form of 're-grief work' which is designed to enable the 'pathological mourner' to revive memories and experiences associated with the deceased, to express appropriate feelings, especially anger, and through testing reality to accept the loss and to develop some ability to live independently of the lost person (see also, Volkan, 1970 and 1971; Volkan and Showalter, 1968).

We know that while most bereaved people will generally recover from a period of intense grief after approximately six months, some may exhibit forms of atypical grief. These include chronic, delayed, and exaggerated or distorted features of normal grief reactions. Such people may be so severely incapacitated in their ability to maintain relationships and to function normally in response to social expectations that they require psychiatric help. What, then, is known about the factors which may alert us to the increased vulnerability of certain individuals or groups? It has been suggested that separation and loss in the early years of life may predispose individuals to some forms of depressive illness later on. Brown *et al.* (1979) conclude, on the basis of a carefully

controlled empirical study, that of past losses (those occurring prior to two years before the onset of depression) *only*
the loss of a mother before the age of eleven years, is associated with a greater risk of depression both among women
treated by psychiatrists and those suffering from depression
in a random sample. However, past losses which occurred
through *death* of a significant other, were associated with
psychotic-like depressive symptoms and their severity, and
other types of past loss *not* involving death were associated
with neurotic-type symptoms and their severity, no matter
at what age the separation took place.

Evidence concerning loss in childhood whether through
divorce, other disruptions in family life, or death of a parent,
and its possible association with later disturbed behaviour, is
complex and often inconsistent. However, when attention is
given to the *quality* of parental relationships and the occur-
rence of family discord, a clearer picture emerges. Rutter
(1972 and 1976) concludes from a thorough review of empirical studies, that while an association has been demonstrated
between parental divorce or separation and conduct disorders
and delinquency, no such association or only a non-significant
trend has been established in the case of parental death and
such behaviour. Rutter accepts that parental death may play
some part in the development of particular disorders, but
concludes that 'delinquency is mainly associated with breaks
which follow parental discord rather than with the loss of a
parent as such' (1976, p. 167).

Rutter examined the findings of several relevant studies
in order to consider the proposition that separation *as such*
may not be recognised as significantly influencing the development of childhood disorders because its effects are only seen
in adult life. He notes evidence from three studies which suggest an association between childhood bereavement and
depressive illness in adulthood, a further three studies which
have found such an association only in cases of severe depression, and four studies which have *not* been able to demonstrate any relationship between childhood bereavement and
functional disorders in later life. What evidence there is, seems
to suggest that bereavement during adolescence is the important condition which may affect the development of disturbed

behaviour later on. Given the finding that parental death may be slightly associated with delinquent activities, Rutter considers whether parent—child separation may be important in this respect. As Rutter points out, however, there are many factors associated with parental death other than separation as such, which may have some bearing on subsequent adjustment. These include the emotional stresses of coping with a long illness, grief reactions of the remaining parent, and financial and social difficulties contingent on the loss of a father. Schowalter (1975) also suggests that parents' failure to help children understand the finality of death and confused communication about what has happened to the lost person, may have a detrimental effect on later development.

Tallmer (1975, p. 164) has asserted that 'the empirical evidence and recent research in the area of childhood bereavement that has surfaced in the last three decades has been fairly extensive and indicates that loss of a parent in childhood augers poorly for adult adjustment'. Simple and categorical statements such as this are misleading. As I have shown, evidence about this matter is inconsistent. The significance of loss is a complex problem and must take into account all the associated factors related to separation, the quality of parental interaction, experience of subsequent nurturing relationships, the circumstances of loss, and the practical difficulties of maintaining family life, before even tentative conclusions can be reached. I have suggested that social workers have a professional responsibility to locate and use available knowledge. It is equally important that they should avoid the assumption of knowledge where there is no consistent evidence to warrant such a position.

In summary then we should be cautious about attributing disturbance in later life to childhood bereavement. There is, however, sufficient and consistent evidence which suggests that particular categories of individuals may be emotionally and socially vulnerable in the event of a bereavement. These are young widows with children, individuals who are already socially isolated or whose support networks become ineffective in the face of death (Maddison and Raphael, 1975), those who may be discouraged from expressing their grief or have no opportunity to do so (Maddison, 1968), those who perceive the death as sudden and untimely, people who have experienced previous mental illness, particularly depressive conditions or other crises occurring close to the bereavement, and those who have had a strongly ambivalent relationship with the deceased. There are, of course, other individual factors such as genetic make-up and personality which are likely to influence the nature of personal grief reactions. However, the broad indicators outlined above provide some clues about those groups of people who may need help in coping successfully with their loss.

A word about the family

Most empirical studies have focused on individual experiences of grief and mourning, particularly with regard to widows and widowers. There is some limited but useful evidence relating to factors which are likely to influence a family's reaction to the death of one of their members. Vollman *et al.* (1971) found that families having open and effective communication systems which facilitated the expression and sharing of sadness, anger, guilt, and so on, were more likely to make a good adjustment following bereavement, than other families with a pattern of denial or suppression of feelings. The family's ability to reorganise significant roles so that family functioning could be maintained, depended on the importance of tasks previously carried out by the deceased. In all cases, however, reallocation of tasks and effective role performance were handled better in families where flexibility and individual skills determined these arrangements. Commenting on the work of Vollman *et al.*, Goldberg (1973, p. 402) concludes 'it would appear that families with a good communication system as well as prior equitable role allocation respond most adaptively to the crisis of death'.

Cohen *et al.* (1977, p. 225) also conclude from their own research that 'the more family members were able to communicate with one another, to share information, and to share in decision-making, the greater the likelihood of an effective adjustment during the post-death period'. In relation to Vollman *et al.*'s finding concerning roles previously performed by the deceased, Cohen *et al.* noted that families in which a mother had died were rated significantly lower on effective communication patterns than others. They therefore suggest that death of a mother may pose particular problems of relatively poor communication, with associated difficulties of family adjustment following bereavement. Post-death re-stabilisation was also found to be significantly correlated with the positive use of external sources of help, including relevant agencies and individuals outside the nuclear family. Those families defined as 'centripetal' or 'inwardly centred' were found to make more effective use of external support systems than those which were outwardly focused (a finding opposite to that which was hypothesised to be the case), and they were also rated as coping significantly better with adjusting to their bereavement.

Conclusion

Our knowledge about dying and bereavement is provided by a wide range of empirical investigations carried out by sociologists, medical practitioners, psychiatrists and very occasionally social workers. Studies have varied in their methodology, the intervals involved in retrospective reports, the timing of follow-up contacts, and ways of recording, categorising and presenting data. This is not the place to make a detailed assessment of the reliability and validity of research findings, and readers are referred to the original literature if they wish to pursue this matter. While I have noted some discrepancies between presentation and interpretation of data, it is perhaps impressive that such a variety of approaches have yielded a body of knowledge which can be used to both facilitate our understanding of dying and grief, and to develop appropriate ways of helping the terminally ill and bereaved.

4

Knowledge about Dying and Bereavement: Interpretation

What all of us want is to be set free. The man who sinks his pickaxe into the ground wants that stroke to mean something. The convict's stroke is not the same as the prospector's for the obvious reason that the prospector's stroke has meaning and the convict's stroke has none.

Antoine de Saint-Exupery, *Wind, Sand and Stars* (1939)

In the preceding chapter, I considered one aspect of available knowledge about dying and bereavement: that is, the empirical data provided by research studies. The second aspect of knowledge involves the ways in which we are able to understand or make sense of such data, and concerns us with matters of interpretation and explanation. This undertaking cannot be avoided if social workers are to understand why they adopt a particular approach to helping clients. It is possible to state a number of 'ground-rules' which might govern work with the dying and bereaved, but to grasp these without some understanding of their basis would leave the social worker inadequately equipped when faced with individual reactions or novel situations. The purpose of this chapter is to consider the major theoretical approaches to making sense of grief and mourning. Much of the available literature on this subject is based on a psychoanalytic model. It is important however to note the contribution which a sociological framework can provide in helping us to understand what researchers and practitioners have actually observed when people are faced with a significant loss.

The traditional approach

Most social workers will be familiar with the basic concepts of psychoanalytic theory which have been widely applied to understanding the process of human growth and development, 'pathological' variations in individual functioning, and the critical stages of increasing maturation from birth to old age. Such a framework has guided many social workers in their interpretation of behaviour, and in their efforts to help clients gain insight into their difficulties through the careful nurturing of a client—worker relationship. This approach has also been used in an attempt to explain what happens to people when they are faced with irreversible loss and the way in which they either recover from such an experience or remain so emotionally tied to the lost person that they are unable to make new relationships or face the demands of everyday life. Most psychoanalytic contributions to this subject are based on the clinical study and treatment of depressive illness or emotional difficulties in adulthood. They are not, therefore, designed to provide an explanation of normally observed grief reactions which have been described in much of the research literature considered in earlier chapters of this book. Given that psychoanalytically oriented writers and practitioners have had a good deal to say about understanding reactions to loss and ways of helping those who have been bereaved, it is important to outline the major themes which have emerged from this approach.

Freud's interpretation of reactions to significant loss emphasises different factors depending on the time at which he was writing. However, he consistently highlights the central part played by the investment of libido or psychic energy, and the individual's need to shift and use such energy in making different emotional attachments. Freud suggests that when an individual loses someone in whom there has been a high investment of libido, he gradually comes to realise that self-centred needs and satisfactions can no longer be met

through an attachment to the lost person. Such an attachment must therefore be discontinued and libido withdrawn.
This idea was developed to take account of how the withdrawn and newly available libido might be used. Freud asserted
that the now free and uninvested libido would be harnessed
by enabling the individual to identify with or 'assimilate' the
lost person. If the bereaved individual has a poorly integrated
ego, the process of withdrawing libido from the lost person
and using it to identify with that person, may not proceed
smoothly. In this case the 'free floating' libido may be active
in promoting hallucinations or projections of the lost person
who remains a separate and emotionally charged focus of
attachment and need fulfilment. What Freud appears to be
saying is that paradoxically the individual must recognise the
reality of loss through identification with the lost person.
This process is accomplished by the movement of libido
which must ultimately be invested in some emotional attachment to enable the use and release of energy. Freud's ideas
have mainly been criticised on the grounds that they emphasise regression to an early narcissistic oral phase of development and that libido is conceptualised as a fixed quantity
of energy which must somehow be 'used up' through an
investment in emotional attachment. Lindemann (1944) has
defined grief-work as 'emancipation from the bondage to the
deceased' although he does not explain this by reference to
the withdrawal and reinvestment of libido. He does suggest,
however, that grief-work involves pain since it depends on
recognising the reality of loss in such a way that the bereaved
can readjust to an environment from which a significant person is missing.

Regression

The notion of regression to some earlier stage of development
plays a major part in much psychoanalytic writing. Pollack
(1961) suggests that bereavement may lead to ego disruption
and regression to the early pleasure—pain principle as a deter-
minant of behaviour. When this happens the individual's need
for satisfaction demands the release of excitement and tension.

Such a release is blocked, however, because the lost person is no longer available to provide a focus for the discharge of this energy. Thus, the undischarged tension results in pain. If this pain is repressed and the individual fails to recognise the reality of loss, energy may be invested in fantasies and day dreams so that the lost person continues to exist as a separate and important focus of emotional attachment. The lost person is thus retained through conversation and fantasy and the bereaved individual is not free to make alternative relationships.

Klein's work also emphasises the importance of early development and the danger of regression in times of stress. She suggests that the child's relationship with his mother is characterised by mixed feelings of hate and love, by wanting to destroy and wanting to repair. Thus, while the loss of a mother is likely to induce a longing for her return, this is also accompanied by the child's paranoid fear that he has lost the good object as a punishment for his destructive and angry feelings. Salzberger-Wittenberg (1970), following Klein's approach, asserts that infantile reactions are a normal response to separation and reflect earlier anxiety about losing or destroying the 'good' parent figure. In this situation the child or adult is faced with potential chaos, fear and guilt. She agrees with Klein's emphasis on the individual being alone with his 'internal world', a world which may crumble into disorder and misery at any time. It would seem that any adult facing a significant loss is prone to regress to an earlier stage of development, which is characterised by feelings of guilt about destructive impulses and fear of punishment through separation from the 'good' parent.

Pincus (1976) explores the ways in which dynamics of family relationships are affected by previous losses, and in their turn influence subsequent responses to loss. She suggests that by paying attention to the interaction between family members, it is possible to pick up clues about the ways in which present relationships are determined by 'buried memories' of 'half conscious experiences' of past relationships and events, and the association between these components of personality and reactions to loss. In her discussion of interaction between family members and between client and therapist, Pincus emphasises the part played by projection and identification. Projection is defined as a process by which an individual 'imagines specific impulses, wishes, aspects of the self or internal objects to be located in some person or object external to himself', and identification as a process by which he 'either extends his identity *into* someone else, borrows his identity *from* someone else, or fuses his identity *with* someone else' (p. 26). Pincus refers to these processes as explaining the association between past relationships and experiences, the development of personality, present functioning, and responses to loss. If, for example, an adult has grown up with strong, oppressive parents who did not allow him to develop his own identity and individuality, he may later identify strongly with his wife in the sense of 'borrowing' his identity from her. Following his wife's subsequent death he may be unable to cope with the loss of identity and fail to emancipate himself from this emotional attachment. It is likely that feelings of anger and guilt towards his parents and his wife will further hinder the individual's recovery from bereavement. Pincus would suggest that, since many of these experiences and past and present feelings are likely to be buried in the unconscious and repressed because of their painful nature, the therapist must interpret the significance of what has happened before, in relation to present methods of coping with loss. Like many other psychoanalytic writers Pincus accepts the importance of regression as a reaction to loss. She asserts that bereavement reactivates the fears and anguish of an earlier stage of development. An adult who suffers bereavement may well regress to the child's primitive state, where fear of abandonment and anguish that loss is a punishment for his own badness are considered to be major determinants of behaviour.

How does this help us?

The short answer to this question is, not very much! From the psychoanalytic point of view, loss causes some imbalance in the individual's inner psychic world. The emphasis may be on disintegration of the ego, movement of libido, regression to a child-like state, primitive fears of destructiveness and abandonment or the association between largely unconscious experiences and feelings, personality development and relationships. Even Pincus's insistence that we should pay attention to interaction seems to boil down to the often unconscious processes of projection and identification. Moreover, psychoanalytically based explanations are derived from the study of people who have experienced difficulties in individual functioning and social relationships and cannot adequately refer to any general understanding of reactions to loss.

Following a psychoanalytic model would involve those working with the bereaved in attempting to identify largely unconscious processes and interpreting the significance of these to clients. The bereaved would be helped to understand how past experiences and relationships had contributed to their particular way of coping with loss. Such an approach would emphasise the client–worker relationship as a means of providing interpretations and enabling the client to gain insight into the cause and nature of his problems. Both the theory and practice elements of a psychoanalytic model may be criticised on several grounds. First, the emphasis on disequilibrium in the inner psychic world neglects the importance of the social context in which bereavement occurs. People do not live alone with their psyches but are members of families, neighbourhoods, peer groups and work groups. They participate in a number of social networks, fulfil different roles and have individual and shared expectations and values which are influenced by the culture in which they live. Second, form and content of social interaction is defined not only by unconscious processes, but by the very conscious business of understanding each other's meaning, guiding the conversation, negotiating outcomes, working out what is acceptable or unacceptable and so on. Third, behaviour is not only determined by past experiences which may or may not reach conscious awareness, but by plans and intentions which are derived from present experience and the anticipation of future goals. Fourth, the worker who sets out to interpret the client's feelings and reactions may well neglect the significance of how the client himself perceives his situation, and the meaning of loss as a social as well as an intrapsychic experience. These points will be developed later in this chapter when attention will be given to an alternative model which takes into account both the social character of loss and the societal context in which it occurs.

What about instincts: an alternative approach?

Bowlby argues that psychoanalytic theory has attempted to explain personality functioning by working backwards from observations obtained in a clinical setting. He suggests that a more useful approach, and that adopted as the basis for his own explanatory framework, is provided by an investigation of how children behave in particular situations. From these data Bowlby developed his well-known description and explanation of attachment behaviour, and responses to separation and loss.

Bowlby's model emphasises major concepts of behaviour systems, feedback and behavioural homeostasis, in such a way as to explain the basis for initiation and termination of behaviour. This explanation rests upon the contention that a new-born baby is already equipped with several behavioural systems which are ready to be activated by specific stimuli falling within one or more broad ranges. Once activated, behaviour systems can develop through interaction with the environment and important figures who inhabit it, particularly the mother. I am less concerned here with the mechanisms by which attachment behaviour actually develops, than with the basic view that behaviour systems appear to comprise related, organised, and directed forms of *instinctive* behaviour. Instinctive behaviour is considered to be that which is environmentally stable and which functions to safeguard survival, particularly by protecting the individual from attacks by predators. Given the premise that instinctive behaviour is adapted to the environment, Bowlby concludes that the 'environment of evolutionary adaptedness' is that which humans inhabited up to the 'past few thousand years'. The development of Bowlby's ideas concerning attachment behaviour is thus fundamentally based on 'elemental responses originating in bygone times'; that is, a repertoire of behaviour systems mediating instinctive behaviour which assured survival in a particular kind of environment. Bowlby further asserts that attachment behaviour in adults is 'a straightforward continuation of attachment behaviour in childhood'. The importance of instincts in relation to attachment, also informs Bowlby's interpretation of separation and loss.

Bowlby's work may be interesting but does not provide us with a great deal of help in either understanding responses to loss or knowing what to do about them. While humans may be viewed in relation to an environment in which they have to survive, there is little exploration of their *social* activities or the importance of their social (as opposed to instinctual) relationships with others. People do not only live in an 'environment' but in a society. If we are to come anywhere near understanding the nature of loss, and more particularly of bereavement and mourning, it is essential that we should explore the social context in which they occur and the meaning which they have for individuals and groups. The central questions which must be given attention are the ways in which individuals construct and interpret their social reality and interact with others in a social and symbolic world.

Social reality

Berger and Luckmann (1967) observe that we live in a world which has some degree of order and stability, and which may be viewed as both objective and subjective reality. Objective reality is that which confronts the individual as an external and taken-for-granted fact. Berger and Luckmann's analysis of society as objective reality concentrates on the ways in which human beings construct a social order which becomes independent of any particular individual's actions. Thus, habitual actions become typified in the sense that we know that certain kinds of actions will have certain results in certain situations. When people interact on the basis of typified patterns of habitual actions, institutionalisation occurs. Since such actions can be dissociated from individual actors, they become part of the 'stock of knowledge' available to all and are readily accessible and amenable to transmission through 'an objectively available sign system', most usually language. When

actions and actors become typified within the context of a
'stock of knowledge' it is possible to recognise roles. Roles
are types of actors who perform types of actions, and can
thus be comprehended without reference to a particular individual. In this sense they are anonymous. Thus when we talk
about a nurse or a policeman we immediately know what
kinds of activity such roles typically entail, whether or not
we are personally acquainted with an individual nurse or
policeman. While the institutional order is only constructed
and maintained by people, it comes to be viewed as having an
external and objective reality which is present before an individual's birth and continues after his death.

Individuals are born into a society of roles and institutions
which are essentially objective and anonymous in character.
These are known and understood through access to a historically sedimented 'stock of knowledge' which is transmitted
through the manipulation of symbols, particularly language.
This reality constitutes the taken-for-granted, everyday
world in which people go about their business. It exists as the
paramount and continually available reality unless anything
happens to call it into question. In this sense it is an objective
reality and allows the individual to live without constant fear
of chaos or disorder (see also Schutz and Luckmann, 1974).

Berger and Luckmann point out that there must be a process of induction, through which an individual comes to
internalise the taken-for-granted reality of the social world.
Initially the definition of objective reality is mediated through
its presentation by significant others, usually parents. Berger
and Luckmann emphasise the importance of cognitive learning
and the emotional basis of identification for the child's inter-
nalisation of objective reality. During this process, the self
develops as a 'reflective entity' internalising the form and
content of addresses by significant others. The child is
gradually able to shift his understanding from particular and
individual actions to types of actions and the nature of roles.
In this way, suggest Berger and Luckmann, the identification
of self and the identification of a general other, that is society,
become separated and defined. Later on, the individual
acquires role-specific knowledge which will enable participation in society on the basis of reciprocal and mutually understood types of actions. The taken-for-granted reality of the

world as it is both subjectively experienced and objectively apprehended, is continually confirmed and maintained through social interaction. The individual's significant others occupy a vital position in confirming both his own subjective reality and identity, and the reality of the objective world. Daily activities and conversations take place in a world that is taken-for-granted, and are guided by shared knowledge and language. In summary, 'identity is formed by social processes. Once crystallised, it is maintained, modified or even reshaped by social relations' (Berger and Luckmann, 1967, p. 194).

While Berger and Luckmann have considered the construction of reality in relation to society, Berger and Kellner (1970) suggest that such processes are at work in smaller units of social interaction. Marriage is one sphere in which reality is constructed and validated. It entails the shift of significant conversations from two realities to that shared by husband and wife, and enables them to construct a subjectively meaningful 'sub-universe' of reality which is not imposed upon them by the institutional order. In marriage each individual's definition of reality must be related to the other's, and thus their experience of themselves and the world will be modified through interaction. Berger and Kellner insist that it is not a case of each individual remaining **the same in a different kind of relationship, but a transforma-** tion of reality and identity. This new and particular reality is developed and maintained through conversation between the marriage partners. As the conversation continues, the shared reality begins to develop a stability and the two individuals' previously separate biographies come to assume a joint memory and history.

Antoine de Saint-Exupery catches something of this process when he says 'life has taught us that love does not consist of gazing at each other, but in looking outward together in the same direction'. There is no suggestion that the construction of a shared reality is an easy business and some marriage partners may find it an impossible task.

Interaction and meaning

While Berger and his associates have attempted to demonstrate how society may be viewed as both objective and subjective reality, symbolic interactionsists have concentrated on the nature of action, interaction and meaning. In summary, Plummer (1975) defines three core ideas of symbolic interactionism. These are first, that man inhabits and creates a symbolic world. Through manipulation of language, symbols and gestures he can interpret and give meaning to objects and actions around him, and can create a world which is subjectively meaningful to both himself and others. Plummer says 'man's ability to make, modify and manipulate symbols is the distinctive feature that makes him truly human and social' (p. 11). Accepting the limits of roles and institutions (and indeed of biology) man may be seen as continually revising and negotiating meanings, through interaction with others. Second, the construction of reality is a *process*. Thus, rather than explaining actions as arising from pre-given instinctual equipment, personality, emotions, and so on, or as a response to external demands, attention is focused on the interpretation and negotiation of meanings through social interaction and the ways in which people make sense of the world around them. Third, individuals cannot be fully understood in terms of any internal psychic or instinctive systems, but only by reference to social interaction.

In relation to these three points the individual not only recognises others as sharing his own world and reality, but is able to become an object to himself. This notion is based on the 'Me' and 'I' aspects of the self. The 'Me' aspect is that which pertains to the individual's previously developed and stable history and includes the 'stock of knowledge' shared by other men and a grasp of roles and typifications which are socially defined. The 'I' is the source of immediate and innovative action. Natanson (1970) suggests that, 'the Me is the source, then, of what is typical and habitual in the experience: the I, of what is innovative and audacious.' Because the 'Me' is historically grounded, it is also constituted from the typified attitudes, actions, and so on, of the generalised other. In this sense the self recognises and shares in an inter-subjective world. As Plummer remarks, 'any human activity involves an individual not only intentionally initiating action, but also imaginatively reconstructing the anticipated responses of others to that action' (p. 17).

Social reality, dying and bereavement

In the preceding section on social reality, interaction and meaning I have attempted to provide a framework in which dying and bereavement can be understood as social experiences rather than intra-psychic events. This discussion can now be specifically developed in relation to the issues associated with death and loss.

Cultural factors

We know that dying and bereavement take place in a social context in terms of organisations, professional definitions of role, social interaction and social meaning. It should be no surprise, therefore, to discover that different cultures manage the problem in different ways. Historically the management of mourning has changed within western society from a mode which specified dress, behaviour, the limits of interaction and the period of time which was considered appropriate for the public expression of grief. Gorer (1965) has suggested that present-day difficulties in coping with bereavement are largely due to the lack of established ritual and structured patterns of mourning. Yamamoto *et al.* (1969) have shown how in Japan, the practice of ancestor worship enables widows to maintain a sense of the presence of the deceased and his continuation through the ancestor family. While accepting the objective reality of loss, these widows were able to maintain a subjectively meaningful link with their dead husbands through the family altar. The disruption of reality, meaning and identity was less severe in such a situation. Ablon (1971, p. 337) comments about reactions to bereavement in a Samoan community, that 'culturally determined attitudes towards death and misfortune serve to mitigate the severe grief reaction that we in America consider to be normal'. The meaning of death is socially defined and the nature of grief reactions and mourning are influenced by the social context in which they occur.

Social interaction

Some studies have shown that the severity of grief is related to the intensity of interaction which the bereaved previously enjoyed with the deceased and the significance of the lost person in terms of vital role fulfilment. It has also been noted that even when relationships were previously ambivalent, intensity and continuity of interaction are likely to result in the expected grief reaction. As Marris (1974, p. 33) correctly notes, 'the intensity of grief is related to the intensity of *involvement*, rather than of love'.

In her study of parents' reactions to stillbirth, Cooper (1980) remarks that it was 'tempting' to expect the grief reactions of shock, denial, isolation, anger, bargaining, depression, confusion, and finally acceptance. She found that the outstanding reaction was one of shock and anger that something which should have been relatively 'safe' and straightforward had gone so badly wrong. While couples were also depressed about their experience, the acute sense of hopelessness and lack of purpose found in other forms of bereavement appeared to be less apparent. These findings are entirely consistent with my approach. The disruption of intense and continuing interaction with significant others results in a breakdown of reality, meaning and identity. If the loss involves a stillbirth or a relatively young child, there may be anger at the injustice and waste, guilt about inaction or inappropriate action, and depression about lost expectations or destroyed potential. However, since the lost individual has not, thus far, been a significant member engaged in the social construction of reality and the negotiation of meaning, or a performer of vital roles, the loss will be unlikely to totally demolish the taken-for-granted reality.

Those investigators who have looked at the topic, have also suggested that the availability and responsiveness of the bereaved individual's social network are vital in facilitating successful grieving. Attempting to explain the vulnerability factor of loss of mother before 11 years old in women who later developed depression, Brown *et al.* (1979) suggest that the loss of a significant other deprives the individual of a source of value and meaning and thus engenders feelings of hoplessness and lack of control. Again, it is my contention that only through social interaction can the bereaved individual begin to reconstruct reality and a sense of meaning and identity. It seems entirely plausible, therefore, that if such sources of interaction are not available, any attempt to construct a subjectively meaningful world will flounder.

Finally, we know that one of the long-standing and most difficult aspects of bereavement concerns social isolation, loss of status and loss of role. Roche (1979) through her experience of working with widows and other single people, draws attention to their common problems. They all suffer from a loss of actual or potential roles, definition of status which makes the negotiation of social interaction hazardous in some circumstances, a stigma which is potentially discrediting (Goffman, 1963) and the difficulty of interacting in a context of taken-for-granted reality which emphasises the acceptability of 'couples' rather than 'singles'.

The nature of crisis

So far I have not specifically referred to crisis theory or crisis intervention. This subject has been given detailed attention elsewhere, both in relation to preventive community programmes and individual crises which involve adjustment to marriage, childbirth, death and so on. Rapoport (1970) suggests that a crisis may be viewed as an upset in a steady state, with associated stress and tension towards achieving a new equilibrium. She suggests that three characteristics are generally agreed to denote a crisis as opposed to any other upsetting and stressful condition. These are, first, the perception of one or more hazardous events which constitute a threat; second, a symbolic link between a threat to present needs and previously experienced threats; and third, an absence of known adaptive or coping mechanisms which facilitate effectively dealing with the threat and re-establishing equilibrium and need fulfilment. The implications of coping with a crisis are that the individual is likely to accept and make use of help because usually employed responses are ineffective and defence systems disrupted, and, if immediate help is not available, the individual may resort to inappropriate and mal-adaptive forms of coping as a way of establishing a new equilibrium. In doing so, it is likely that he will be rendered more vulnerable and less able to cope with any future crises. This predicament is illustrated by the bereaved person who denies the reality of loss and thus avoids the pain of what Lindemann (1944) calls 'grief-work'. While maintaining some degree of equilibrium in this way, total disorientation may result from any subsequent crisis which shatters the potentially vulnerable balance achieved at the cost of facing and learning to live with reality.

I would like to elaborate the concept of crisis in line with the approach developed earlier. A crisis may be said to occur when something happens to call into question the individual's taken-for-granted reality and there is no alternative system of meaning which can provide a basis for purposeful action. This poses a threat to the accepted nature of reality itself, to the meanings through which events and self and others are understood, and to the location of self and identity within a potentially alien and chaotic world. Such a crisis may occur at the macro-level through such holocausts as occupation by a foreign power in war or political revolution; at the intermediate level through such events as natural disasters or community disruption; or at the micro-level where an individual is suddenly cut off from those resources which enable continuing confirmation of reality and identity. Or, of course, it may occur at all three levels simultaneously.

Garfinkel (1967) persuaded some of his students to induce a crisis by refusing to respond in the usual way to conversational remarks. Instead of acting towards others on the basis of a taken-for-granted and shared reality, they feigned misunderstanding of the simplest comments, insisted on questioning, and demanded evidence. Interaction rapidly broke down, normal coping mechanisms failed to be effective, and hostility and suspicion prevailed (see also Goffman, 1959, ch. 7). Where reality is disrupted to such a degree, there are no immediately effective coping mechanisms. Re-establishing a viable and stable equilibrium depends on the individual's ability to reconstruct reality, meaning, and a sense of identity out of chaos.

Conclusion

It should be clear that I do not regard psychoanalytic or instinct-based models as providing either a theoretically adequate explanation of reactions to loss or a framework which might generally suggest effective ways of helping the dying and bereaved. Both approaches neglect the significance of what we know about culturally prescribed interpretations of death and institutionalised forms of expressing and managing grief. By emphasising the importance of *internal* psychic or instinctive responses, they also fail to sufficiently explore the nature of social interaction as both influencing responses to loss and hindering or facilitating eventual recovery. The suggestion that responses may be largely determined by unconscious experience and feelings or instinctive systems, ignores the individual's capacity to act intentionally, to plan, to be consciously aware of the meaning of his own and other's actions, and to create and modify meaning through the *process* of interaction. Information from studies of animals has been used to add credence to the instinct-based theories of human behaviour. It is unwarranted to infer the presence of human beliefs and experiences in animals, simply because in certain situations observed behaviour may be similar in some respects. There is no evidence that animals act towards each other on the basis of inter-subjective understanding or meaning and indeed they lack the ability to make and manipulate symbols, particularly language, which would enable them to do so.

Having made the points above, I should add that for some clients and therapists who are working together in a clinical setting, explanations which are derived from a psychoanalytic or instinct model may provide guidance or be acceptable as a helpful focus for developing self-knowledge. However, the aim of this chapter has been to consider a more general framework for understanding reactions to loss and bereavement which is not confined to pathological conditions but which can help us to make sense of people's experiences as they are felt and expressed in our ordinary everyday world. In following chapters reference will be made to individual feelings, perceptions, responses and ways of coping with actual or impending loss. The framework which I have attempted to develop does not ignore or deny the importance of the individual. It does, however, emphasise that an individual functions within a social context and suggests that the focus of attention should be on the meaning of events and experiences as he or she perceives them, rather than on some 'buried' or unconscious history which can only be made available through therapeutic interpretation. What I have suggested is a different way of 'making sense' of the information at our disposal which is based on a fuller and more generally applicable consideration of our knowledge to date. In some cases individual psycho-therapeutic help may be necessary, but the business of social workers is to attend to the socio-emotional consequences of loss and not to concentrate on solitary intra-psychic conflicts.

I have suggested an alternative approach to understanding the significance of loss which emphasises the disruption of taken-for-granted reality, meaning and identity. This firmly places the experience of dying and bereavement in a social context. The practice implications of this approach will be developed in following chapters when I will consider the contribution of social workers in helping the dying and bereaved. However, the theoretical model suggests that in practice attention should be given to the cultural context of loss, the significance of social interaction between the bereaved and the deceased and the bereaved and his social network, and the *meaning* of loss for those involved. It further directs our attention to interaction between social workers and clients in terms of mutual interpretation and negotiation of verbal and non-verbal exchanges.

My own approach is comparable with that of some other writers who have attempted to understand personal and social problems from an interactionist perspective. Marris (1974) has explored the significance of loss in relation to a disruption of taken-for-granted reality and meaning. He suggests that, viewed in this way it is possible to understand not only the nature of bereavement and the response of grief and mourning, but other losses which engender similar feelings of confusion, hopelessness and lack of purpose. Other writers have also discussed the loss of meaningful activity and roles in relation to the problems of middle age, amputation of a limb, and community disruption. Houghton and Houghton (1977) have emphasised the difficulties of involuntarily childless couples and their expression of 'unfocused grief' as a response to the loss of purposeful action, self-esteem, and the anticipated rewards of parenthood.

In the field of social work practice, Leighton (1973) has asserted that social workers should refine their skills in terms of understanding the meaning which individuals ascribe to the social world and themselves as they act within it. Knott (1974) and Fitzjohn (1974) have applied themselves to describing and explaining the ways in which social workers and clients engage in social interaction, with all the interpretation and negotiation of meanings and expectations which this involves.

It is in relation to such aspects of social interaction that bereavement, grief and mourning may be understood. While I did not initially make any reference to this approach in my work with the dying and bereaved, it has gradually enabled me to make greater sense of their reactions and to clarify the ways in which social workers can provide effective help.

5
Working with the Dying

I was perfectly ready to fall asleep, whether for a night
or for eternity. If I did fall asleep, I would not even
know whether it was for the one or for the other. And
the peace of sleep! But that great cry that would be sent
up at home, that great wail of desolation — that was
what I could not bear.

Antoine de Saint-Exupery, *Wind, Sand and Stars* (1939)

Many books which are in one way or another about doing
social work, divide the subject with reference to techniques,
skills, levels of intervention, and so on. I have decided to
avoid that here because it involves jumping between important
individuals and groups, and fragments the process of description and explanation. Throughout the following discussion
it will be possible to identify those particular elements of the
social worker's role which constitute that aspect of knowledge
referred to by Timms and Timms (1977) as 'know-how'.

Self-knowledge

The reader, by this stage, should have some knowledge about
what the dying and bereaved say about their feelings and the
ways in which they are observed to react, and a reasonable
basis for making some interpretations about the meaning of
these data. One of the difficulties about the shift in perspective in this and following chapters, is that data may be

presented and assimilated in a reasonably objective fashion. A discussion of social work techniques and skills for working in this area may be recorded and defined in a similarly objective way. However, somewhere in the middle of all this is that individual who has a professional identity and a professional way of going about a day's work, while at the same time having a personal identity and way of responding to the world. Of course the professional and the personal aspects of self are not that well defined or easily separated. My personal self probably has something to do with choosing social work as a career, and my professional self will probably come to influence the way I think about certain problems and what I decide to do about them. Clients will not only respond to the *professional* presentation of self but also to all those factors associated with social class, cultural background, perceived attitudes, and oft-mentioned qualities of warmth, compassion, sensitivity and so on. It is a mistake to assume that because social workers are trained to fulfil certain role requirements, or because they actually do so whether or not they are trained, they will be perceived in the same way by different groups of clients. Neither does such uniformity of attitude depend on the social worker's ability to provide particular services. My own research concerning the ways in which prospective adoptive parents viewed their interaction with agency social workers clearly illustrates this point (Smith, 1980). While respondents' attitudes were influenced by agency policy and some of the more uniform questions and approaches of workers, many couples expressed unease, annoyance, or anxiety about the proportion of 'career' social workers who either were not parents or who, because of age, marital status, or other characteristics, were considered not to be interested in parenthood. In this situation, prospective adopters suggested that social workers could not understand their feelings about wanting children, were not in a position to advise them, and could not possibly reach valid conclusions about whether they would make 'good' adoptive parents. It was not so much the objective characteristics of social workers which were significant in this context, but couples' feelings that they and their workers were poles apart in terms of aspirations, values, and indeed the meaning of life. Evidence from another source suggests that the relationship satisfaction of interviewees is likely to be significantly greater when they perceive the interviewer as similar in views and life-style preferences to themselves (Tessler, 1975). The benefits of 'matching' clients and social workers according to clients' characteristics and workers' interests, skills, and aptitudes, has also been discussed by Palmer (1973).

While the question of matching social workers and clients has many professional and practical implications, knowledge about one's professional self does not just mean knowing something about techniques and skills. An ability to do the job well also involves being alert to the way in which the client perceives the social worker and his assessment of whether the worker is an *acceptable* source of help. How the client views the social worker will depend on many factors, including whether the client thinks he is getting the help he requires, whether he trusts the worker, and the demeanour of the worker involved. I am not suggesting that it is always practical, or necessarily desirable, for workers and clients to be matched according to any one of a range of characteristics. The social worker should be aware, however, that the client is likely to be making his own assessment, not only on the basis of how warm, concerned, or ready to help the worker is, but also in relation to whether they are likely to have any common ground for understanding each other, differences and similarities between their views of the world, whether they can actually communicate given different language patterns and meanings, and so on. If social workers are alert to the client's assessment and to some of the factors which play a part in this, they will be better equipped to understand those elements of mutual definition and negotiation which will certainly influence the initial phase of any interaction. If a client is silent, indifferent, apparently not expressing something which would help the worker to make sense of his problem, it is not necessarily the case that he is unable to exercise insight or is denying a particularly painful or negative thought or feeling. He may be wondering how a social worker could possibly grasp the meaning, not only of his words, but of his social and personal world. This difficulty may need to be acknowledged if the client is not to give it all up as a bad job, and the social worker is not to decide that she has failed or that the client is simply insufficiently motivated to work towards a solution.

The second important aspect of self-knowledge involves the response of the professional and personal self to dying and bereavement. Social workers are likely to have strong feelings about their work. They may be angry about social injustice, about a mother's difficulty in caring for her child because of poor housing, inadequate income, lack of play space, a dearth of nursery facilities and so on. There are a number of ways in which this anger can lead to constructive action. They may act as an advocate on the mother's behalf and ensure that her case gets a reasonable hearing when it comes to allocating scarce resources, or they may help mothers in a similar situation to organise a play group or draft a petition, or join with the elderly and single parents to argue their common need for a community centre. A social worker may also be angry about the death of a child or a young mother, or depressed by terminal illness which incapacitates and causes pain. When a client asks 'What can it possibly mean?' or 'Why me?' there appears to be no response which can lessen the distress or change the reality to something better. Leared (1978) comments that sometimes it is impossible to say anything which does not amount to denying the impact of hopelessness and chaos. In this situation social workers cannot so readily take positive action to modify or solve the problem. Anticipating, accepting, and controlling the expression of such strong responses is part of the development of self-knowledge. Neither can social workers take comfort from a position of relative privilege and ability to control their social world. Social workers are as vulnerable as clients when it comes to death. If a worker has been bereaved, forgotten feelings and regrets are likely to crop up again during the course of trying to help those who are facing death and loss. Self-knowledge also requires that social workers are able to concentrate on what this situation means to the client(s), and not only on what it means to them in terms of lost opportunities and lost relationships.

The context

I will concentrate here on patients who are dying in hospital, since it is in this setting that much intensive work is likely to occur. The patient may be able to return home for a period, or may have been admitted from home because the illness has reached such a stage that the family could no longer cope. In any event we are considering an individual who has been diagnosed as being terminally ill. Treatment aimed at curing the illness will have been given up, although there may be subsequent tests to check progress and treatment designed to relieve pain. Such a diagnosis may be reached several months before death can be expected and it is often difficult to accurately predict a person's remaining life-span.

Any social worker trying to help someone who is dying must pay attention to the context of intervention. First, there is the organisational context. The efficient running of a hospital depends on the operation of certain agreed and established principles. There must be an orderly routine so that patients are investigated, treated, fed, washed, allowed visitors, and so on, without unexpected disruptions. Porters, nurses, doctors, social workers and other staff members have a role – and so does the patient and his family. Organisationally, there are a number of roles depending on typified actions and actors. Each individual has a good idea of what such roles entail, despite having to learn the intricate details *in situ*. Patients are expected to comply with routine and to co-operate with medical personnel so that their conditions can be investigated and treated. There may be some room for the patient to negotiate his position but this is limited. In terms of power, control, and access to valued resources, medical staff are in a much better position than patients to impose their definition of the situation. It has been noted that the need to maintain an orderly routine may well emphasise the importance of technical competance and the categorisation of patients, illnesses, treatments and problems, rather than relationship capabilities and individualised assessments.

Second, the professional context has implications for how members of professional groups are expected to behave, who is allowed to disclose certain kinds of information regarding diagnosis and prognosis, how the hierarchy of status and responsibility works, who has control over the distribution of resources and decision-making. Although there are some written reports describing how small, multi-disciplinary teams can work effectively in caring for the dying patient and his family, such arrangements appear to be relatively uncommon. In a large general hospital the social worker is likely to be in a marginal position with less clearly defined role expectations, responsibilities, and freedom to make decisions than other members of medical staff.

Third, there is the question of values. Undoubtedly doctors are in a position where they can legitimately impose their value system on other members of staff. This might be related, for example, to the remarkably uniform attitude detected in empirical studies that since it is impossible to decide which patients can cope with knowledge about their terminal illness, information should be withheld from them all. There is also an assumption that the smooth running of the ward will be interrupted if patients are distressed by talking about their approaching death. An overtly distressed patient may upset other patients and nursing staff, take up valuable time, and disrupt routine procedures. This is not to suggest that medical personnel are callous or indifferent, merely to point out that there are inevitable tensions which exist between organisational demands, professional values and responsibilities, and individual needs. As McIntosh (1977) notes in his study, doctors perceived themselves as responding to patients on the basis of individual assessment of needs. However, they were consistently observed to use routine categories of replies for what they regarded as types of questions and types of patients. In this way they avoided the impact of experiencing the patient as a person.

These central elements of the hospital as a context for social work have several implications which must be considered. If a social worker recognises that a patient suspects or is fairly sure that he is terminally ill and wants to discuss practical arrangements, how to help his family, or just to talk about his anxiety and fears, what is the appropriate response? Or if a patient has been given evasive answers about his diagnosis and prognosis by the doctor and his family, and finds uncertainty more frightening than the truth, what does the social worker do? Acknowledging a person's fears and permitting the expression of unhappiness might seem to be appropriate from the social worker's professional perspective, but is also likely to interfere with organisational requirements, the allocation of power and status, and the paramount system of values. I can well remember talking to an elderly lady who would have been at considerable risk had she returned to her upstairs flat as she wanted to do. We discussed her situation from all angles, and in the end she felt that her long-term needs would best be met in residential care. This lady felt sure that this was the right decision, but it did not stop her feeling distressed about her loss of independence and the loss of her home. She had a good cry about it all and we were able to recognise her mixed feelings of relief and sadness. However, such an overt expression of grief caused considerable consternation among the nursing staff who were caring for this patient. She had been too upset to eat and the other patients were worried about her. The nursing staff felt that she should not have been allowed to become so distressed and attempted to calm her down by reassuring her that everything would be alright! In fact, the patient subsequently became less depressed than she had been before our talk, was able to plan for the future, felt pleased that she had made her own decision, and stopped resenting the doctor who had said she could not return home. I was unfortunately seen as someone who was in the business of 'upsetting people', the covert message being that I also had a tendency to upset hospital routine.

Because of inevitable tensions between how the social worker may view her role in responding to patients' needs and organisational requirements, it is vital to attend to the following questions. First, how is the social worker viewed by medical personnel? Is the social worker seen as someone who will exercise a control function in line with organisational needs by reassuring patients about the future and dealing effectively with any worrying problems about finances, care of children, housing, and so on? If patients are not anxious about what is happening at home or at work they are more likely to co-operate with treatment, avoid making a fuss, and to be less disruptive. Second, how are the social worker's responsibilities defined in terms of relative status and decision-making? Must all questions about discussion of diagnosis and prognosis with patients be referred to the doctor? Third is the social worker viewed as a colleague with complementary knowledge and skills or only as someone who facilitates the doctor's role by clearing beds of elderly patients, arranging transport and organising home-helps?

In my view, there is likely to be a tension between the expressive, affective and cognitive elements of the social worker's role and the instrumental, clinical and routinised aspects of doctors' and nurses' roles. I do not wish to draw this distinction too strongly because Parsons's notion of 'affective neutrality', universalism and functional specificity as characterising the doctor's role, has been criticised on several grounds. However, I think it needs to be recognised if social workers are not to unwittingly disrupt taken-for-granted routines and engender hostility within a hospital setting. There is a challenge here for social workers if they can fulfil some of those affective functions which pose a particular problem for medical staff. In order to do this the social worker must attend to organisational and professional constraints and develop ways of working skilfully with colleagues, or with what Pincus and Minahan have called the 'action system'. There are various ways of achieving this.

First, the social worker must apply herself to assembling data about the way an organisation functions. This can be done by spending time on the wards, attending meetings and ward rounds, talking to medical staff. Through listening and observing, the social worker will become aware of some of the routine assumptions and responses of medical staff, particularly in situations which engender uncertainty and anxiety.

Second, by being present during discussions about patients, the social worker can pick up problems as perceived by medical staff and suggest possible ways of managing these. For example, I was attending a meeting where a doctor expressed concern about a patient who would not co-operate with medical staff. She would not eat, was hostile, and would not answer their questions about how she was feeling. This was upsetting nurses, making treatment difficult and generally interfering with the atmosphere and orderly routine of the ward. I asked for a little more information about this patient and discovered that she was young, suffering from acute ulcerative colitis, and had two children who were being cared for by her mother-in-law. This woman had pleaded with the doctors to let her go home and they had flatly refused. The doctor said that if she went home it would interrupt her treatment and the pressures of looking after her husband and children would probably exacerbate her condition. There had been no room for negotiation. I suggested that she might be particularly worried about what was happening at home, and that her lack of control might well be increasing her anxiety. It was agreed that I should talk to the patient and report back. When I did talk to this woman, I discovered that she perceived her mother-in-law as a powerful and competent person who had effectively taken over her role and assumed responsibility for her husband and young children. Realistically, she was worried about re-establishing a relationship with her children, her loss of role fulfilment, her lack of control over events, and her lack of power to influence decisions about her own body. I concentrated on finding out how this patient interpreted her situation. In other words, what did it mean to her? When I reported back to the medical team, I suggested that it would be helpful for this woman to return home for a long weekend in order for her to establish that she could still function as a wife and mother and to allow her some power and control. They were doubtful, but I undertook to interview her husband to explain the situation and to investigate the likely effectiveness of her social and support networks. The patient did go home for the weekend and when she returned she resumed a co-operative attitude, responded to treatment and was soon discharged. There was no miraculous outcome here. The patient had been defined as a 'difficult woman' who refused to comply with typical requirements of the patient role, whereas by concentrating on how she perceived her situation, it was possible to improve both her sense of control and her relationship with medical personnel. Following her weekend at home, this woman was happier and more settled and from the doctor's point of view she stopped disrupting treatment and ward routine. In such a situation, I was able to facilitate organisational and professional requirements and as such became seen as a potentially useful member of the team.

Third, if the social worker picks up a reference to a patient's difficult behaviour, it may be possible to offer some explanation both of the behaviour and of the ways in which reactions of medical staff may exacerbate the problem. Stockwell (1972) has shown how nurses typically react to demanding, critical or unhappy patients by imposing sanctions. Such sanctions include, ignoring them, forgetting their requests, using sarcasm and refusing to talk to them. For a patient who is confused and unhappy and does not know how to ask for help or how to engage medical staff in acceptable conversation, such difficult behaviour may be a plea for attention. Frequently it appears to have the opposite consequence to that desired, by increasing isolation and diminishing self-esteem. In this kind of situation the social worker can take direct action by talking to the patient and/or increasing the understanding of medical staff by drawing their attention to the processes involved.

Fourth, the social worker should ensure that there is effective communication about what the patient knows, proposed action and likely outcome. In the case of someone who is terminally ill, the social worker will need to know the routine explanation which has been given to that person by medical staff, anything the patient has said which might give a clue about his feelings or suspicions and whether he has appeared withdrawn or angry. The social worker must then clarify that in the event of some indication from the patient that he knows he is unlikely to go home or that he is dying, acknowledgement can be given. A report should always be made to nursing staff, particularly if a visit to the patient has encouraged or allowed some expression of distress.

Fifth, the social worker should be available, not only to patients and their families but most importantly, in this context, to nurses and doctors. It is no good allowing a dying patient the opportunity to share his fear and worry and to express his grief, if the social worker then disappears and leaves everyone else to pick up the pieces. It is vital that the social worker is seen to be aware and in control of her own feelings, and not to be embarrassed or afraid of the fundamental issues which have been made explicit. In relation to routine management problems, it is also necessary for the social worker to take responsibility for following through contact with a patient. Nurses and doctors should not be expected to cope with the consequences of a social worker's intervention, and are likely to be angry if this interferes with carrying out their own professional responsibilities.

Sixth, throughout the points outlined above there runs an educative and explanatory role for social workers. Nurses and doctors can directly observe the beneficial results of social work if it helps them to do their jobs more effectively. Where it causes difficulties and conflicts with the requirements of organisational and professional values, explanation and good communication are vital. Doctors and nurses may wonder why someone is angry with them when they have done their best to protect them from distressing information, or why a person who acknowledges that he is terminally ill at one moment later talks about where he is going on holiday next year. If medical staff work with an implicit frame of reference which emphasises typical and rational aspects of attitudes and behaviour, they may be upset or respond inappropriately to a patient who behaves in this way. Explanations can be given during individual contacts with nurses and doctors, or it is sometimes possible to arrange a team meeting around a specific problem, such as care of the dying. A bombastic approach, as in any situation of social interaction, is likely to arouse resentment. However, if the social worker tries to comprehend these difficulties from the point of view of medical staff and respects those areas in which they have to take responsibility for making decisions, it should be possible to encourage joint learning and shared understanding. Negotiating skills and a recognition of potentially conflicting interests provide a good basis for beginning.

Seventh, it will inevitably happen that negotiation sometimes fails. I was working with a patient who, following an accident, was paralysed from the neck down. Medical opinion was that he would not recover, that the limits of treatment had been reached, and that as he lived alone he would have to move into some form of long-term institutional care. This man was confused and panic stricken. No one would talk to him about the diagnosis and prognosis, and the nurses avoided him because of his obvious distress. Not only had he suddenly lost his taken-for-granted life-style, roles and expectations, but he was beginning to lose any sense of himself as a thinking, planning person who could exert any control over what would happen to him. His difficulties arose, not only from his enormous losses, but from his inability to negotiate and a pattern of interaction where normal expectations of communication had broken down. If he asked a question about the future, he was told that everything would be alright, everything would be taken care of, or he was not to worry; in effect his questions were never answered. His sense of reality and ability to ascribe meaning to his own thoughts and actions were rapidly becoming attenuated. He was treated as though he, as a person, did not exist. My job was to try to keep this patient from disrupting the ward, since he was continually demanding nurses' attention, upsetting other patients and being unco-operative. However, I was supposed to carry out this task without acknowledging this man's distress or talking about what concerned him most. I tried all my techniques of persuasion and explanation, but the consultant insisted that the patient would only be more difficult if he was told the truth. The consultant would talk to him when he considered it necessary. In this situation, nursing staff recognised the patient's needs, but neither they nor I could do anything about them. Balancing this person's distress against my future ability to help other patients on the ward and the prescriptions of the hierarchical system, I complied with the consultant's decision. Sometimes one has little alternative where professional relationships are defined by relative power and status.

The comments above do not mean that I think social workers are, of necessity, more sensitive or more concerned about patients than are doctors or nurses. However, it would appear to be difficult for medical staff to combine a role based on technical (caring) skills and typifications of patients and their illnesses, with one which emphasises individuality and social and emotional areas of functioning. The social worker is in a position to help both medical staff and patients by being aware of, and doing something about, the person who also happens to be a patient.

The dying patient

Where a person has been ill for some time, there will usually be a number of clues about his condition which he may pick up if he wishes. The nature of his treatment will have changed; he may have caught friends or relations in an attitude of sadness only to be answered with false brightness when he inquires what is wrong; he may be aware that his illness seems worse than before; or people may simply avoid him. Reassurances are empty to some people, while to others they present a life-line which is eagerly grasped. As an illness progresses the patient may be moved to a separate room, doctors will probably visit less often, people with whom he has been on easy terms will suddenly appear tongue-tied and embarrassed. If a person is able to accept the truth, it is usually there for him to see. If he prefers not to do so, he will interpret what goes on around him in the most acceptable way. The patient, like every client, is the social worker's best guide regarding how to proceed.

The interview

A patient may generally be referred to the social worker for two reasons. Either he has expressed some particular concern about work, his family, finances, and so on, or he may be demanding, difficult, or withdrawn. Whatever the reason, it is important as in any interview to give some thought to where it should be held. A terminally ill person will probably not be able to go far and it is likely that the interview will have to be conducted at his bedside. Since hospital organisation is typically not concerned with such activities, it is vital to think ahead. The arrival of someone coming to take a blood sample in the middle of an interview is obviously not conducive to a successful meeting. It is easy to forget such details in the course of a busy working day, but nursing staff can be helpful in making necessary arrangements or allocating an office to facilitate privacy if the social worker is able to plan ahead. Much has already been written about the characteristics of social work interviews. We know that they should be purposeful, structured, and have a beginning, a middle and an end. It has also been noted that not all clients know what social workers do, or what to expect, and that it is therefore the worker's responsibility to help a client define his requirements, agree goals, clarify the steps which will be taken towards achieving these, and guide the progress of interaction. Cross (1974) has pointed out that the basic skills required for interviewing are purposiveness, emphasis on individuality, and emphasis on common themes, the last factor referring to social and cultural perspectives of interviewer and interviewee. Since these aspects of social workers' and clients' interaction have already been explored in great detail, I will concentrate here on those issues which are particularly relevant to working with those who are dying.

The beginning

If the social worker has been asked to see a patient who has expressed concern about a particular problem, there is a starting-point for interaction. The worker should be sure to leave the way open for the patient to express any other anxieties by saying, for example, 'I understand that you are worried about . . . and I am here to see if I can help you with this . . . or anything else that may be worrying you.' In any interview, an ability to listen carefully, to observe and to recognise cues is important. Since our main concern here is with finding out if a person wants to acknowledge that he is dying, wants to talk about this, or wants to make specific plans for the future, the way must be left open for him to do so. Several other conditions must also obtain. The social worker must demonstrate through her manner that she is prepared to share these problems with the patient. Avoidance techniques may predominate when a social worker is aware that she holds information about diagnosis and prognosis which the patient does not have, when she feels sad for the patient, or if she is alarmed about the possibility of mutual disclosure of such information. The social worker may sit at a distance, avoid eye-to-eye contact, be very formal, look uncomfortable, and so on. Someone who wishes to discuss a specific and concrete request for help may merely think the social worker to be rather odd and unfriendly. This is enough to make any client diffident about discussing what concerns him and expecting that the social worker will do something about it. He may therefore minimise the importance of the problem, stop talking, and fail to enter into any agreement about achieving goals. For a patient who suspects or recognises that he is dying, this approach will immediately warn him that the social worker wishes to avoid the issue. At the beginning of the interview, the social worker should therefore adopt an attitude both verbally and through her whole manner, that illustrates a willingness to engage the client.

It is important to remember that the patient will observe and interpret a social worker's communication and actions. The worker's initial approach will provide the client with vital clues about what he can subsequently expect. By placing an emphasis on interaction I intend to remind the worker that what goes on during an interview is reciprocal. Any client will attempt to grasp the meaning and to 'make sense' of social exchanges. If he is also aware that he is dying, he is likely to have in mind some specific questions. These will probably be; does the social worker know? Is she embarrassed or upset by the knowledge? How can I spare her feelings? Should I raise the subject or will it frighten her off? How can I find out if she is trustworthy? The patient is therefore likely to attend carefully to any cues from the social worker that she is, or is not, prepared to discuss the matter. The beginning phase of the interveew may well be characterised by exploration and initial negotiation about the form and content of acceptable communication.

The middle

Discussion will proceed about the patient's expressed concern.

As usual the social worker will help to clarify the nature of the difficulty, set priorities, and agree a course of action. It may be a relatively simple matter regarding a wife's difficulty in visiting because she cannot get a babysitter, or a query about financial benefits. If a patient is returning home and lives alone, it may be a question of organising a home-help, a volunteer service, or a good-neighbour scheme, to visit, do the shopping, possibly collect the pension, and so on. Patient and social worker may need to decide whether the former can manage at home at all, and social networks will probably need to be explored to assess members' ability and motivation to help. Or a patient may be worried about returning to a damp house or an upstairs flat and the social worker may decide to discuss the matter with the housing department and try to arrange medical priority for a change in accommodation. If the social worker is listening and observing carefully and is alert to the possibility that there may be a 'hidden agenda' which concerns the patient's terminal illness, the interaction may develop in a number of ways. The first possibility is that the patient appears reasonably relaxed, in so far as he thinks that some action will be taken to ease his worries. He will concentrate on the subject being discussed and give the social worker sufficient information to enable a plan to be agreed. There is no hint that he either knows about or wants to discuss his terminal illness or approaching death. If this seems to be the case, the interview will remain focused on the acknowledged problem.

The second possibility is that the patient knows or suspects that he is terminally ill and either wants to talk about it, or just wants to have the fact acknowledged so that he can avoid the strain of keeping it to himself and protecting everyone else. In this case, he is likely to present a number of cues to 'test the water' having already assessed that the social worker is at least open to such an approach. The patient may say something like: 'There must be some reason why I haven't got better'; or 'I feel so tired after all this illness but my family keep saying I have to get better'; or 'My wife keeps saying she's expecting me home, but I won't be going'; or 'I'm worried about my children having to grow up without me.' Now, with the best will in the world, the social worker may baulk at getting into such potentially deep water and may not know how to respond. Another set of avoidance tactics may come into play if she is not prepared for this. They may be subtle – a slight change in expression denoting embarrassment or alarm, or a physical movement away from the patient. Or, they may be more obvious – a reminder that they were just discussing the rent, a continuation with the conversation as though nothing had happened, a cheerful denial, shuffling of notes, looking around for help, and so on. Faced with such a response, the patient may be embarrassed because he realises that he has misread the social worker's ability to cope with this, or distressed because it appears that another channel for sharing his fears and hopes has been closed. The interview may break down unless the social worker can rally the necessary resources to say, 'I'm sorry but you took me a little by surprise', or 'I'm sorry, I was just thinking about the rent but you sound as though there may be something else which is worrying you.' Bearing in mind that the patient may not want to discuss this area but just to have it accepted, or that he may be doing the 'ground work' to find out if he can rely on the social worker when he does want to talk about it, this is probably not the time to jump in at the deep end. However, we do know from evidence already presented, that the patient would be unlikely to make such remarks if he preferred to pretend that he was on the road to recovery and would be going on to lead a long and healthy life.

The best way to proceed then, is to show that the way is still open for the patient to change the course of the interview or to talk about his major area of worry. The social worker's attitude of attentiveness, concern, confidence and continuing physical proximity will give the patient important cues about how to continue. The social worker may also say something like: 'Has anyone talked to you about your illness or how things are likely to go?'; or 'It's only natural for your family to want you home and to push doubts to the back of their minds'; or 'What makes you think you won't be able to see your children grow up?' At some point the patient may say that he knows about his illness, and the social worker can quite naturally ask if he wants to talk about it. If the patient does want to discuss the matter there are a number of topics which might be worrying him, and I will consider these in detail later.

The third possibility is that the patient may continue to talk about the recognised problem, but be thinking about his terminal illness. He may not be quite sure whether he wants to mention the subject at all or whether the social worker is an appropriate person with whom to raise the matter. The social worker may notice that the patient is fidgety, avoids eye-to-eye contact, appears not to be following the conversation, or conveys by his tone of voice that he is unhappy. In such an event, the social worker can ask if there is anything else which is worrying him, or comment that he looks unhappy or preoccupied with something else. If he replies that he is alright, it is possible to confirm that the social worker is always available if anything else crops up which he would like to discuss. The fourth possibility is that the patient will raise the subject of terminal illness quite openly and the social worker should be ready to respond without embarrassment or anxiety.

Ending the interview

If the interview has focused primarily on the recognised problem, the social worker will make sure that she has all the necessary information, that agreement has been reached about action to be taken, and an arrangement made for the social worker to report back. In the event of an interview turning to the patient's concern about his terminal illness, a number of areas will probably have been discussed. Specific difficulties might have arisen from this discussion about which further decisions need to be made. If this is the case, then the usual process of agreeing goals and action and making arrangements to report back should occur. Whether the patient's illness is tacitly acknowledged without further elaboration or considered at some length, it is vital that the social worker should arrange to see the patient again. This provides reassurance that the social worker is not going to be 'frightened away' by the patient's condition, and that there will be

another opportunity to talk about the subject if he has not felt able to do so on this occasion. If the patient has discussed his fears or been angry or distressed at this meeting, it is also important for him to understand that this is acceptable and in no way affects the social worker's willingness to see him again. While it is always important that clients should not be left in limbo, a terminal patient's fear of isolation and relative powerlessness makes this particularly significant. It lets the patient know that he is not devalued or avoided because of his illness and it establishes the social worker's trustworthiness and continuing concern.

The social worker may try to bring the interview to a close on the basis that a problem or related problems have been clarified and a plan of action agreed, or that a second interview is required to explore the matter further. Every social worker is probably familar with the client who raises a potentially painful area just as the worker is leaving, or tries to delay the worker because some difficulty still remains unexpressed. A terminally ill person may use such tactics, and if the opportunity is not to be lost the social worker must be willing to discuss the problem before she leaves. If she simply does not have time, or as is likely, it looks as though the interview may become extended, the social worker can acknowledge that she understands the patient may want to talk about the matter more fully and arrange a subsequent interview as early as possible. If the worker has shown that she is not uncomfortable in this situation, she will be trusted to come back.

If a patient has been referred because he is demanding or withdrawn rather than because he has voiced a particular problem, the social worker may begin the interview by saying that nursing staff are concerned that the patient seems to be unhappy and she wonders if she can help. The same kind of negotiating may go on concerning what topics may or may not be discussed and similar verbal exchanges may occur. Once again the patient should be helped to perceive the social worker as attentive, concerned, and confident and the social worker should provide verbal and non-verbal indications that this is so.

Several points should be noted at this juncture. It is not

the case that every person will know or want to know the precise nature of their diagnosis and prognosis, so it should not be assumed that their major concern is specifically to do with terminal illness. However, if the social worker attends carefully to the cues which she is given and shows that whatever is worrying the patient may be safely acknowledged, the danger of leaving a patient socially isolated and afraid may be avoided. The patient may not wish to discuss his terminal illness but may want reassurance that the social worker is available should he want to do so later, or simply that someone is prepared to accept the situation with him and to recognise his individuality through the expression of personal concern. In this event, much of the communication may be non-verbal. The social worker may only say something like: 'I think I can understand how difficult it must be for you'; or 'I think I can understand how you might be feeling.' If such a short statement is accompanied by confirmation through eye-to-eye contact, close proximity, or if it seems appropriate actual physical contact, the patient will know that the social worker has grasped his need to share the problem. The patient may want no more than that.

It is also important to remember that the maintenance of hope is important to terminally ill patients. This means that any communication may not relate to dying or death, but to the fact that someone has a serious illness which cannot be cured at present. The 'escape clause' for a patient may be the hope that he will beat the illness, that further treatment may become available, or that doctors have been overly gloomy in their assessment. It is thus possible for a person to talk about their diagnosis of terminal illness while at the same time referring to some indefinite future, or to recognise that recovery is unlikely without explicitly linking this information to the process of dying. Or, a patient may refer to *his* illness and dying *in general*, expressing his feelings about death but at one step removed from anticipating this as a personal experience. What may be expressed in terms of 'what will happen when I'm gone', at one time, may be replaced by 'I'm feeling much better and will be able to go home soon', at another. Changes in emphasis and interpretation may be understood as reflecting a person's struggle to cope with the difficulty of being alive 'now' and not wishing to abandon the meaning of activities and relationships, and at the same time being aware that the threat of loss is real and possibly imminent. In order to maintain a sense of identity, the patient can not continually anticipate a state of 'not being' (Das, 1971). He therefore has to balance the knowledge that he is terminally ill against the business of actually living his life in the present and defining projects and plans for the future. In such a situation, a recognition that the future is limited must sometimes be put into 'brackets', in order to allow continued social functioning. Putting knowledge or feelings into 'brackets' in this way is not equivalent to burying them in deeper layers of consciousness, but suggests that the patient wishes to turn his attention to other matters. The importance of this for the social worker is that the activity of careful listening and observing cannot be abandoned. A social worker must always be alert to all the elements of interaction, and cannot expect that expression of feelings or sharing of knowlege will proceed in an orderly fashion. It is extremely difficult, if not impossible, to know in advance which 'type' of patient can explicitly consider his own death. Close attention to the individual is the only way to discover what the patient is prepared to acknowledge, and when he may wish to 'bracket' his awareness for the time being.

Some patients may protect themselves from having to face the possibility of terminal illness by simply not asking about the diagnosis or prognosis, or by answering the question themselves. I can remember an intelligent single woman who had failed to seek medical advice about a lump in her breast. When she began to feel really ill she consulted her general practitioner and was admitted to hospital immediately. By this time cancer had spread so extensively that nothing could be done. While this woman gradually became more ill, she never ceased to maintain that feeling worse was a prelude to getting better. At times, however, her tone of voice or the expression in her eyes clearly gave away her lonely and desperate feelings. I did not think that this woman wanted her precarious balance to be upset by making her fears explicit. What I could do was to ensure that she would not be isolated and I spent time sitting with her and just talking about whatever she introduced, or saying nothing. It is sometimes the ability to be concerned, and always to look at and sit close to someone, that lets them know they have an ally and will not be left alone when they are afraid or in despair.

A social worker may wonder whether her liking for a patient or her own feelings of vulnerability will hinder the kind of interaction which I have described. Despite the concern that a client will know what the worker is feeling, there is evidence to suggest that what the worker says and how she behaves will largely shape the client's perceptions. The worker's attitude will be conveyed by verbal and non-verbal communication. If self-knowledge is something which has been given sustained attention, the worker should be aware of significant factors in her presentation of self and be able to differentiate the way in which she responds to a client from the way in which she may be feeling.

What will the patient want to discuss

Having considered various ways of tackling an interview with someone who is terminally ill from the point of view of our central concern, I want to discuss the form and content of subsequent interaction. How might it help a dying person to acknowledge or talk about his situation with a social worker? I have already mentioned the importance of tacit understanding, where although explicit discussion of dying may not occur, there are no false attempts at cheerfulness and the patient is allowed the relief of being sad without being alone. Alternatively, the patient may just wish to talk about all his mixed feelings of anger, confusion, fear, and so on. It has been noted that those who are terminally ill are often conscious about upsetting others, concerned about causing embarrassment, worried about protecting their family from distressing experiences, and subject to being socially and emotionally isolated. The opportunity to simply express themselves to someone who is perceived as being reliable and trustworthy is often a great relief. By reliable here, I mean someone who can be depended upon not to retreat in embarrassment or emotional turmoil. By trustworthy, I mean someone who will not make judgements about a person's expression of anger or lack of self-control, and who will continue to be concerned and keep promises to return.

A person who is dying is likely to express a flood of feelings once he is permitted to do so. He may be angry with the world in general or with particular people. Questions like, 'Why me?' or accusations that 'Nobody cares', or 'It's not fair', or 'It should have happened to someone who's had their life', are likely to express the patient's feelings. The social worker does not have to say a great deal at this time. Being able to tolerate such remarks while maintaining an attitude which communicates that it is alright and the worker is not going anywhere, is sufficient at this stage. When a patient is angry, any attempt to say 'I know how you feel' may be realistically perceived as trivialising the patient's distress. How can a social worker with a promising future and the ability to control her life 'know' how it feels to face the total disruption of everything that has been taken for granted and the enormity of impending loss? Ironically, the social worker represents what the patient has lost or is going to lose — health, emotional and physical strength, control, confidence, the ability to fulfil a role and plan for the future. While the patient wants to talk to someone who is sufficiently sure of their own identity and place in the world not to be overwhelmed or embarrassed, these very characteristics reflect his own loss. Any attempt at verbal reassurance is likely to exacerbate this inherent conflict.

When a patient is angry, the social worker can help in several ways. First, the worker is someone who can tolerate and understand this anger. Members of the family may have been confronted with anger or irritability. If they have not been helped to consider the reasons for this they will be hurt and confused, and may respond in a negative way by withdrawing their social and emotional resources. Medical staff who are faced with hostile or demanding patients have been shown to react by using strategies which further engender social isolation. The social worker can accept that a patient is likely to be angry, can allow the patient to express his feelings, and can reassure him that this is normal and understandable. Second, the worker can explain that it is difficult for nursing staff and relations to tolerate anger because they themselves are worried about the patient. This may seem obvious, but caught in a spiral of hostile interaction the patient cannot be expected to 'see through' the anxieties of others and to make allowances for these. Once it is explained that everyone feels vulnerable and concerned about saying the right thing, the patient will begin to see that he can still exert some control over the situation. Third, the worker can explain to medical staff and the patient's family that such anger is natural, not personally directed, and related to feelings of frustration and powerlessness. Once others can be helped to see that the patient is not realistically angry with *them*, the spiral of increasing distance and mutual recrimination can be halted. Fourth, the patient will be aware that he is breaking accepted rules for reciprocally rewarding social interaction, that in spite of himself he is terminating rather than enhancing social exchanges. Such awareness, although it may not be explicitly recognised, is likely to diminish an attitude of self-esteem and social competence. By listening, maintaining concern, and continuing interaction, even if this is only by physical presence or a nod of the head, the social worker can help a patient to maintain some sense of his own value and individuality.

At some time the patient will be sad and depressed about his condition. I would suggest that any social worker needs to ask herself what the whole situation is likely to mean to the client. Looked at from the patient's point of view, terminal illness generally involves loss. We are used to the idea of loss in relation to those who are bereaved, but probably give it less attention in trying to understand the dying. The patient is already likely to have suffered a loss of power and control, a loss of role performance and a loss of self-esteem. His taken-for-granted reality has crumbled and he no longer has the power or independence to modify this. Terminal illness does not represent a hiccup in the construction of reality, but a full stop and the need for a reassessment. A great deal of difficulty can arise when a patient perceives that his reality is out of step with the taken-for-granted world of everyone else. When he asks a question which is not answered, when he expresses concern which is ignored or cheerfully dismissed, when significant others carry on as though everything is normal, the patient becomes 'locked-up' with his own reality and progressively more alienated from the 'outside' world. In such a situation the social worker should first, recognise the patient's reality and by doing so continue to confirm his sense of identity and self-esteem; second, act as a bridge between the patient and others and help to bring their realities into line; third, while acknowledging that reality for the patient has drastically changed, illustrate ways in which he can still play a significant part in shaping and confirming a shared reality with others.

Recognising the patient's reality indicates that the social worker should face his losses with him, and avoid the often frequent denials which he will receive from others. The patient should be allowed to be sad about what he has lost without being told to cheer up, or to stop being morbid, or made to feel that his sadness is upsetting everyone else. By acknowledging the importance of what he has to say and being interested, the social worker can confirm a person's sense of identity and self-esteem. The worker should not be afraid to ask questions or seek clarification during such a discussion, since this encourages the patient to feel that what he is saying is worthwhile; that he, as an individual, still has something useful and interesting to say about his life. If the social worker can explain the patient's social isolation to others and assure them that he will not lose control or become thoroughly depressed if they acknowledge his feelings, they can be helped to bite their lips before false reassurances are uttered. If they can acknowledge the reality and meaning of loss for the patient and enter into a dialogue with him, not only will they begin to inhabit the same social world, but through continued interaction they can construct a social reality which is shared rather than individually exclusive and mutually isolating.

Constructing a new social reality not only involves talking about the same thing and coming to a mutual understanding of the situation, but also negotiating certain important changes which are related to terminal illness. Consider a relatively young man, about 50 years old, who had run his own business. While he was in hospital his wife had taken over much of the work, having previously helped him in an assistant/ secretarial capacity before his admission. She protected him from any participation in business affairs, fearing that this would make his health worse. In order to effect his compliance she was always cheerful, promising that when he came home she would let him get on with it. This patient was angry and frustrated with his wife for several reasons. First, she would not recognise his terminal illness, the likelihood that he would be unable to run the business for long, or the need to plan realistically for a future without him. Second, her insistence that he could look after the business when he returned home effectively debarred him from having any role (except that of patient) while he was in hospital. Third, his sense of identity and self-esteem were being eroded because his wife would not recognise or talk to him about his major concern and denied that there was anything seriously wrong. Fifth, he could not express his sadness or his regrets to the most significant person in his life without disrupting the reality which she was trying so hard to maintain. If someone clearly wishes to deny the terminal nature of his illness, then the reality which he perceives may be in line with that of his family and friends and there should be little difficulty. However, in the case just described communication began to break down because the patient and his wife were carrying on separate conversations in the context of mutually exclusive definitions of reality.

In this situation, the social worker was able to show the patient that his wife was not being uncaring or trying to deprive him of vital functions so that her power and control would be increased at his expense. She was, however, attempting to protect him, and in some sense herself, from having to make the drastic transition which was required. With the patient's permission the social worker talked to his wife and interpreted his reality to her, including his knowledge about his terminal illness, his response to this, the losses which he had already suffered and the way in which he perceived her activities. Once this had been done they could both acknowledge the terminal illness, and begin to bring their perceptions into line. When the patient's wife began to understand the meaning of her husband's condition she could appreciate that she was increasing his sense of loss. From then on, the wife brought some work into the hospital which her husband could do and they worked on some aspects of the business together. The patient's sense of control and self-esteem increased and they were able to plan for the future. As this example illustrates, the social worker can help to confirm a patient's identity through personal interaction. Where possible she must also enable the patient and his significant others to understand the change in reality and the meaning which this has for everyone involved.

The patient will also anticipate certain losses as he moves towards death. There are lost opportunities, the things he will not be able to do and things he regets having done but can no longer change. There is the loss of family and friends (Aldrich, 1963) and the lost pleasure and responsibility in helping his children grow up. At this time the dying person may well wish to review what has happened during his life. There are often small incidents or worries which seemed relatively unimportant at the time and had been forgotten, but which assume significance in the face of terminal illness. The patient may be concerned about lies, misunderstandings, or arrangements which he put off making. When time is short he may feel that it is imperative to put such matters right. The patient may hesitate to mention forgotten incidents to family and friends, or if he does so they may respond by dismissing his worries as 'morbid' or 'out of proportion'. The social worker can convey to the patient that she understands the importance of putting things right when there will be no opportunity to do so 'some time later on'. Through discussion with relatives and friends she can also help them to comprehend the meaning of loss and the urgency of achieving some degree of order and harmony in response to impending death.

The dying person may experience a conflict between hoping that important people will not be distressed by his death, but fearing that he will not have made a lasting impact on their lives and will soon be forgotten. The social worker cannot change the situation or make good the losses, but she can acknowledge that they are significant to this individual. In stressful situations, people may often dwell on the negative aspects of their lives. It is only by expressing their doubts to someone else that these can be put into a perspective which illustrates that everyone's life is a mixture of success and failure. By attending carefully to this individual the social worker implicitly confirms the patient's value as a person and can help him remember the positive experiences, relationships and achievements which may be lost amid the regrets. The objective is not to say 'of course you did the right thing', or 'or course you could not have done anything else', or 'you must not think you have failed' but to confirm that this person as an individual, probably made the same mistakes and attained many of the successes which are shared by most people. He is valued for himself and for his unique contribution to the social reality which he constructed with others.

As a patient moves closer to death, he may be ready to give up the hard work involved in staying alive. Social interaction becomes less important and the patient may not want to talk, joke, or take any responsibility for maintaining social exchanges. It is at this time that quiet reassurance and an ability to understand the patient's withdrawal, are vital. It is distressing for a patient who is tired and who has had enough, to be reminded that he has in some way a duty to keep fighting, not to let his family down, and to be chivvied back into a social world which he is ready to give up.

Often family and friends cannot understand that someone can or should stop fighting to stay alive, and may interpret the patient's readiness to die as a personal abandonment. Once again, the social worker can explain that this is a common reaction and not a personal rejection, and help significant others to appreciate reality from the patient's perspective. When patients are near to death, medical staff may try to protect family members by suggesting they leave and asserting that the patient is 'no longer aware of their presence'. When they are tired and confused, relatives may be unable to counter this suggestion or may feel ambivalent about being with the patient at the time of death. However, I have often heard relatives express regret when they realise that they left the patient to die alone. Nursing staff can be made aware of this and encouraged to ask relatives what they would like to do instead of making the decision for them. When a social worker knows the family and they need reassurance and support while they sit with a patient, it is helpful if this can be given. I once waited with a woman while her husband was dying. Her rising panic was evident from her expression and the tension as she gripped the side of the bed. All I had to do to help her was to calmly squeeze her hand. This was enough to remind her that she was not alone and that whatever happened there was some stability and continuity in her life.

It is not my intention to suggest that *only* social workers can give this kind of help, but that they should have the necessary self-knowledge, confidence, and ability to respond appropriately, which would enable them to be effective helpers in this context.

Spiritual help

It should be clear from the foregoing discussion that it is difficult to talk about working with terminally ill patients without making some reference to their interaction with others. Thus, at some point, it becomes imperative to work with nurses, doctors and members of the patient's family, in order to improve their understanding of the patient's reality and the meaning of terminal illness. Since dying is likely to involve the spiritual meaning of life and death, consideration should be given to the role of the clergyman in this context. Freund (1977) suggests that many people may be resistant to asking a clergyman to see a dying patient and recognises that historically there may be an understandable reason for this. However, he also asserts that the clergyman may be able to help in several ways; he can acknowledge impending death rather than joining those who isolate the patient through denial; he can encourage the patient to express anger at God and help to ameliorate the guilt and fear which this may engender by emphasising that 'God is bigger than our anger'. He may be able to help a patient talk about his fear that God is punishing him through inflicting illness, and get such worries into perspective. As Kübler-Ross (1970) has noted, some patients will bargain with God in an attempt to lengthen their lives or escape death. A clergyman may be the most appropriate person to discuss the meaning of this activity and the guilt which is associated with approaching God in this way. Freund also suggests that a clergyman's life will have been 'dedicated to searching out meanings' and that he may therefore 'be more attuned than most to the struggle and process of arriving at meanings' (1977, p. 214).

With reference to 'self-knowledge', any social worker in contact with a dying patient should be aware of her prejudices concerning the role of religion and her attitudes towards the clergyman as a source of help. Not all patients will find a clergyman's visit either relevant or helpful. However, some people derive comfort from religion or may have become particularly aware of the spiritual aspects of dying and questions about what will happen following death. A clergyman may well provide a source of reassurance, clarification and spiritual comfort which social workers find more difficult to convey. I recall a middle-aged woman, who following considerable hardship in her own life, had argued with her local minister and subsequently stopped attending church. She had felt that her minister did not care about her, that he was only concerned with the ritual of worship and that if God was content to allow this state of affairs, she had had enough of Him and His religion. As this woman approached death she expressed considerable conflict regarding her wish to reaffirm her belief in God, to accept spiritual comfort, and her feeling that she had rejected Him and did not deserve any help. Finding myself out of depth with this kind of problem, I asked the hospital Chaplain to visit. He was able to reassure this patient that God would have understood her feelings, that because all human beings are vulnerable and make mistakes they sometimes 'lose touch' with God, and that the spiritual comfort which she sought would gladly be given. The patient was greatly relieved and attained a peace of mind which allowed her to die without a struggle.

Using groups

Discussions about social work with the dying have largely assumed the necessity of a one-to-one relationship between the worker and client. While this can provide the basis for effective help, the use of group discussions can also be beneficial. Although this method of working is widely used in other settings, little attention has been given to the advantages of helping the dying through such an approach. Goodyear (1977) has described the use of groups in helping advanced cancer patients. The initial reason for trying to help patients in this way focused on their feelings of isolation and personal bewilderment. It therefore seemed appropriate to find a way of enabling patients to see that they were not alone with their fears and physical problems and encouraging them to share many of the strong feelings which terminal illness engenders. In addition to this, it was hoped that patients would be motivated to explore the reality of their present situations and to assess how they could make better use of the time which was left. Through making relationships with other terminally ill patients they could express worries and fears which family and friends might find difficult to grasp and develop a continuing source of support outside the formal group meetings.

Goodyear describes the group discussions as developing through three clearly defined stages. First, patients expressed their confusion and anger, often complaining that others found them 'frightening', could not cope with their strong feelings, and therefore avoided them. It would appear that their anger had reached boiling point as a result of the social isolation which they experienced. Goodyear notes that all the group members expressed their fear of losing emotional and intellectual control. They referred to the continual conflict between accepting and denying their illness, a difficulty which was exacerbated by the clearly anxious and ambivalent attitudes of family and medical staff. The second stage, defined in terms of indecision, moved from expression of anger to a recognition of fear and the frustration and sadness of loss. By the third stage of acceptance, patients were beginning to look at the personal impact of their illness, practical issues of managing interaction with medical staff, and the ways in which they tended to react to people and situations, both before and during the period of terminal care.

It appeared that the group provided a setting in which

patients could spontaneously express their feelings without fear of a dismissive, anxious or punitive response. This had previously been difficult, given the constraints imposed by expectations of the patient role and organisational procedures, and the responsibility of managing interaction with friends and relations. Patients had reached the stage where they were not only angry about being ill, but angry and confused about the reactions of those around them. The stigma which may attach to the bereaved also seems to present difficulties for those who are dying, by blocking or distorting social interaction and eroding their ability to maintain a sense of identity and self-esteem. It was only after patients had been enabled to express these feelings and then to work out how far they were realistic and how far they reflected personal anxieties and expectations, that they were able to look more constructively at ways of controlling their environment and managing social interaction. Group discussion facilitated this process because all members shared the same social reality and the same discrediting or potentially discrediting stigma (see Goffman, 1963). They were thus released from the tension which was imposed by the actual and anticipated reactions of others and were able to develop strategies for coping with other people's behaviour. All these activities increased an awareness of their ability to exert some control in social situations, and in association with this their sense of power and self-esteem. Goodyear remarks that although members appeared to derive considerable benefit from group meetings, this was only possible when the therapist had been able to confront the personal impact of being close to dying people and associated feelings of anger and despair. She says, 'ultimately, each member must face death alone, and the therapist's task of continually considering this factor and her own death was often anxiety provoking' (1977, p. 249).

Conclusion

Compassion and concern are vital prerequisites in any attempt to work with dying patients. However, it is the expression of these attitudes through words and actions which are likely to guide a client's assessment and willingness to accept help. Obviously, compassion and concern are not the sole property of social workers to the exclusion of nurses, doctors, friends, family, the ward orderly, or anyone else. But the development of relevant knowledge and skills and the distribution of responsibilities between professional groups means that social workers are in an advantageous position to help the dying patient and his family. Social work emphasises knowledge about, and practice in, social situations, with attention to the form and content of social interaction (see also Kadushin, 1972). Basic principles of social work practice highlight the importance of a client's individuality, self-determination and right to respect *as a person*. The methods employed in practice comprise assessment, planning, and use of resources towards attaining a particular goal. Techniques include the ability to attend to verbal and non-verbal communication in such a way as to grasp the meaning which such exchanges are intended to convey. I have used the word 'attend' here to indicate that the social worker listens in a particular way, and is alert to the process of social interaction which involves the negotiation of meanings, the recognition of cues and mutual interpretation of actions. Understanding reality and meaning are therefore focal concerns of social work practice and require cognitive as well as affective application.

Working with the dying patient thus involves several areas of knowledge and practice. In terms of the context, a social worker must have knowledge about organisational requirements, professional role differentiation and value systems, and must be able to intervene in difficult situations, clarify and explain, communicate effectively, and be available. In relation to the patient, a social worker must have self-knowledge concerning personal attitudes to dying and loss, presentation of self and an awareness of spiritual interests. The worker should be perceived as reliable, confident and trustworthy and be able to recognise cues, encourage expression of feelings, avoid denial, accept anger, recognise the patient's sense of loss, clarify and explain to the patient and others, allow the patient control, and enhance feelings of identity and self-esteem. It is commonly suggested that people who are dying regress both physically and emotionally. Physical regression may be unavoidable, but the struggle to maintain a sense of purpose and control will be frustrated if the patient is treated in a way which denies his reality and identity. It is much more likely to be the difficulties of care-givers which influence a patient's ability to maintain a sense of power and independence, than the experience of being terminally ill as such. Perhaps the greatest contribution of social work in this context is to recognise these inherent dilemmas and, through paying attention to social exchanges, to help each individual maintain a sense of identity and self-esteem in the face of total loss.

6
Working with the Dying Patient's Family

I realised clearly that something extraordinary was happening. I was holding him close in my arms as if he were a little child; and yet it seemed to me that he was rushing headlong towards an abyss from which I could do nothing to restrain him.

Antoine de Saint-Exupery, *The Little Prince* (1945)

The first encounter

When I began working with the families of terminally ill patients, my knowledge and professional confidence were in the relatively early stages of development. The doctors who had become concerned about this area decided that something had to be done. With little idea of what exactly this might be, they handed the whole problem over to their social worker. Despite the progress which we had made in recognising the existence of a problem, we made little constructive effort to work out a team approach. Doctors maintained their responsibility for telling the family that a patient was terminally ill and I subsequently received shocked and confused relatives in my office. It became clear that medical personnel had little idea about how to communicate the news of terminal illness. They were kind and as gentle as possible. However, they frequently moved on from disclosure of diagnosis and prognosis to suggest that plans should be made for the patient to return home as soon as possible. Since nothing more could be done to aid recovery, the organisational and clinical requirements for discharge of patients and clearance of beds became a matter of immediate concern. Difficulties arose over the use of medical terminology, misunderstanding of communication, failure to ask questions and confused expectations.

In this context, it is worth noting Lonsdale's (1979) discussion about the way in which a team approach enabled doctor and social worker to see couples together when giving information about the birth or physical deterioration of a handicapped child. The social worker was able to monitor communication, help the couple to ask relevant questions, and be available immediately afterwards to help them sort out their feelings, clarify the situation, and begin the task of assessing what should be done next. I would suggest that wherever possible, doctor and social worker should both be present when relatives are informed of a patient's terminal condition.

Expectations of the initial interview can only be limited, whether the social worker is actually present when information is given or sees relatives shortly after. Relatives are likely to be shocked and numb, and to have difficulty grasping the finality of diagnosis and prognosis. The immediate reaction is usually one of disbelief. Similar kinds of desperate assertions tumble out – 'It can't be true', or 'I can't believe it', or 'He must have made a mistake!' So concerned are relatives to grasp the significance of what they have been told, that they review their conversation with the doctor in an effort to bring some kind of order out of the chaos. The nature of interaction between relatives and doctors is usually so circumscribed by factors of power, status, diffidence, and expectations of appropriate behaviour, that the former will probably have acted in a controlled and rational manner throughout the interview. Social workers' actions can be differentiated from those employed by medical personnel in certain important respects. The social worker should avoid acting in such a way as to heighten awareness of social distance and professional status. Using techniques for the maintenance of social distance may be legitimate for doctors, whose business is to impart information as clearly as possible. It is not, however, appropriate for social workers whose aim must be to recognise and allow the expression of confusion, anger, grief, and so on. The social worker should free relatives, for the moment, from normal social expectations governing appropriate role-related behaviour. This may be achieved by a number of simple manoeuvres. She may go to greet relatives, guide them immediately to a chair possibly with brief physical contact, say she is sorry that they have had such bad news, and acknowledge that they must be feeling shocked and confused. The manner of engaging individuals demonstrates that the social worker is concerned *for them* and is not afraid or embarrassed by their inability to conform to acceptable patterns of social interaction.

Initially, the social worker should allow time for the relatives to grapple with their confusion while gently reinforcing the information that they have been given. If the worker can express an attitude of concern and confidence, while at the same time refusing to confirm any false hopes that it is all a mistake, relatives will soon confront reality. They may then be overwhelmed by fear, anger and panic, often all at the same time. As long as the social worker shows no sign of being alarmed or embarrassed and says simply that it is acceptable and normal to express such feelings, relatives are allowed the release of tension which may be difficult to attain in other situations. Considering the worker's relationship with older children who are being placed for adoption, Neilson (1979, p. 89) suggests that 'no child was ever hurt by seeing tears in a worker's eyes, if at the same time he knew that the worker had things under control'. I do not wish to suggest that adult relatives regress to a child-like state. However, given the universal nature of actual or potential loss, any intense expression of distress may prompt an emotional response from the social worker. I would agree with Neilson, that such a response is not necessarily detrimental if the social worker recognises her responsibility to maintain control and to help individuals bring some degree of order to their feelings and experiences. During this initial contact, the social worker has the delicate task of maintaining a balance between personal engagement which permits the expression of strong feelings, and professional confidence which provides an assurance of order and reliability. Much of this is achieved through the social worker's demeanour, rather than what is actually said, and depends to a large extent on the worker's ability to maintain an attitude of concern, acceptance and tolerance. Once again the worker's awareness of her own reactions and presentation of self, are vitally important.

The expression of grief and anger will eventually subside. Relatives will often apologise as they calm down sufficiently to recognise that they have ignored the normal rules for social interaction. The social worker should say clearly that there is no need to apologise and that she understands and accepts their need to 'let go'. At this juncture, the social worker should impose some direction on the interview, since relatives will still feel too confused and upset to articulate their main concerns. The worker should ask if relatives think that they understand the information which they have been given. She will often find that there is minimal comprehension and that there are many unasked questions. These usually focus on the expected course of the terminal phase, how the patient's physical abilities can be expected to deteriorate, whether and when he will suffer pain, what kind of nursing care will be needed. In association with these questions there arises the problem of home management and worries about what will happen if, and when, the family find they can no longer cope. These problems should not be tackled in the initial interview for several reasons. First, relatives and social worker are likely to be tired by the intensity of feeling which they have shared. Second, even if the worker has shown tolerance and understanding, she is still a comparative stranger and time is needed for relatives to regain some composure and sense of control. Third, relatives can not be expected to organise their thoughts or consider the future in any positive way when everything which was taken for granted has suddenly fallen apart. The social worker should therefore deal with immediate problems concerning diagnosis and prognosis, by either undertaking to talk with the doctor or arranging to take relatives to see the doctor again and being present to help them articulate their major questions. The worker should also ensure that a further appointment is made within a few days to discuss problems of caring for and living with someone who is terminally ill. I emphasise that appointments should be made with relatives or with a dying patient at the end of an interview because this demonstrates in a concrete way that the social worker is trustworthy and reliable. It is also common for relatives to leave their first encounter with a social worker with many unfocused questions and worries which will only become apparent when they get home and have time for the information to sink in. If they know that there will be another opportunity to discuss these problems at a specified time, this will do much to allay their fears and prevent the debilitating effects of panic. It is also helpful to remind relatives that if they have any pressing worries or want to talk to the social worker before their next meeting, they should not hesitate to telephone. These are simple suggestions. However, unless we remember the isolation and confusion which result from a disruption of reality and meaning, it is easy to forget that relatives will be living through this over the next few days and may need the reassurance of knowing that a social worker is available and represents a stable reference point in an otherwise chaotic world.

I should add a word of warning here. In setting out to describe the reactions of family members, it is necessary to refer to general observations of behaviour. It should be remembered, however, that people will come to their interview with the doctor and social worker from a variety of social backgrounds, with varying degrees of ability and social-support networks, and with different perceptions of their relationship with the terminally ill patient. While they all face impending loss, the meaning of this experience will have changing implications for different people. Unless the social worker pays careful attention to this question of meaning, she may fail to grasp the significance of what has happened for the particular individuals who are involved. There are common themes which may guide the social worker when preparing to meet relatives, but she should not underestimate the importance of attending to each individual's response. The major question which must be confronted, is what does this information *mean* to the individual in terms of his reality and the social context in which he lives?

The second interview

Relatives are likely to come to this interview with many questions and worries which have caught up on them since their last visit. There is thus a danger that the discussion will move rapidly from one actual or anticipated worry to another, with social worker and relatives becoming confused and failing to work out an orderly plan. This is unfortunate for any client who seeks help in a bewildering and distressing situation. For those who are facing loss and whose ability to maintain an awareness of order and meaning is tenuous, it is vital that someone can be relied upon to provide a framework in which the client can make sense of what is going on and what can be expected. The responsibility for providing order and direction must fall to the social worker. Since it is necessary to gain some idea of pressing concerns, relatives should be invited to tell the worker what has been worrying them since the last interview. It is likely that the worker will be presented with a number of related issues and questions. Common difficulties are:

1. Coping with the patient at home: causing unnecessary suffering; fears that if the patient is discharged he will not be readmitted; facing death.
2. Answering the patient's questions about deteriorating health: protecting him from the truth; lying and dishonesty in relationships.
3. What to tell the children and other family members: managing social interaction.
4. How to live with anticipated loss: the disruption of reality and meaning.

When working with clients who express several overlapping problems and who are confused and overwhelmed by the perceived enormity of their difficulties and inability to sort out priorities, the social worker's immediate task is one of analysis. She must break down the apparently insurmountable series of problems into manageable parts before any constructive work can be done. In the context of terminal illness, the most pressing question is whether the patient should go home and this is likely to present a source of panic for many relatives. The doctor is likely to have presented the patient's discharge as something which should be arranged as soon as possible, and since then relatives will probably have been assailed by conflicting advice about whether they should comply with this proposal. The social worker may be the first person with whom relatives can sit down and discuss the matter without the pressure of doctors' expectations or friendly but ill-informed advice.

The social worker may thus say something like: 'There are obviously a lot of things which we need to talk about, but your most pressing worry seems to be about taking the patient home – do you think we should start off with that?' Having defined the problem to be discussed and with information about difficulties commonly experienced while caring for a dying patient at home, the social worker should consider several areas. First, how do relatives feel about this? There may be various practical worries about pain control, nursing, lifting, staying up all night, and so on. The house may not be suitable, have poor facilities or an outside toilet. The patient may not yet have reached the stage where he will have to stay in bed and worries about what will happen in another six months may come crowding in. It is important for the social worker to explain that additional help can be arranged. Although the availability of resources will vary between areas, the social worker should be sufficiently well informed to advise on night-sitting services, sheet-laundering services in the event of incontinence, help from voluntary groups, the loaning of a commode, Department of Health and Social Security allowances for special diets. The simple expedient of arranging for a commode to be loaned or for sheets to be laundered can make all the difference between a potentially overwhelming burden and one that can be adequately managed. Relatives should be assured that the social worker will discuss any problems with the appropriate services and will provide direct help if they are diffident about asking general practitioners or district nurses for pain-relieving measures or nursing assistance. It then becomes at least possible to contemplate whether they would like to care for the patient at home. One of the greatest fears is that relatives will be abandoned by medical and social services to struggle on alone, and that in so doing they will mishandle the patient's care and cause him pain and distress. If the social worker can describe the kinds of support services which will be available, and more importantly, ensure that they are put into operation and their effectiveness assessed at regular intervals, relatives should not be left in the situation which they most fear.

Having come this far, relatives will have a much more realistic appreciation of the practical issues involved in home care and how far they can be resolved. The difficulties should not be underestimated. If, however, relatives know that they can continue to call on a social worker to discuss problems and gain help in dealing with outside agencies, they are much more likely to make a decision based on a positive desire to care for the patient than one which is primarily influenced by confusion and fear. While relatives may conclude that they feel ready to cope with the patient's return home, they can only do this if they know that difficulties are anticipated and agreed plans have been made. When I was working with families of terminally ill patients or with patients who lived alone, it was possible to warn the Marie Curie Memorial Foundation Hospital that the patient would probably need a bed within an approximate period of time. The Marie Curie Hospital was a terminal-care home designed for patients who did not need the investigative and treatment resources of a general hospital. I discussed the availability of beds in this establishment with relatives and gave them information about the experience and concern of staff who cared for terminally ill patients. Many relatives were reassured that arrangements could be made for the patient's admission if they reached the point where they could no longer cope. Others were concerned about the nature of the hospital. If after further discussion their fears remained or admission was simply impracticable because of travelling arrangements, it was important to agree with a responsible doctor that if necessary the patient could be readmitted to the present hospital. It is only possible for relatives to consider what they are able to do in the immediate future within a framework which ensures that they will not later be left alone with an overwhelming problem. If this is not appreciated, fear of the future can intrude into any ability to make present decisions. The social worker must thus help relatives to consider the range of present choices on the basis of realistic information and within the context of a reliable plan for the future. Once relatives are given time and a focus for their disorganised thoughts without the demand for immediate discharge, they are much better able to order available information and to come to their own conclusions. It is not surprising that once relatives have rediscovered their ability to organise information and events, to work out possibilities and to plan for the future, some sense of meaning and personal control begins to return. They are then able to begin thinking about related issues with more confidence.

By beginning the interview in this way relatives are able to grasp and work on a fairly concrete problem. The social worker is able to show that something effective can be done to help. This is important because it demonstrates that relatives are still able to order their lives and make decisions, and that the social worker can help to influence the course of events preceding death. The fact of impending loss is unchangeable and people must be helped to find a balance between accepting this and living their lives in a purposeful way. Jointly, social worker and relatives can begin to establish a working relationship which reflects this balance and depends on constructive effort, rather than the expression of sympathy on one hand and the feeling that life is meaningless on the other.

Living with someone who is dying presupposes social interaction. It seems that relatives usually approach this problem on the basis that the patient does not know about the terminal nature of his illness and that he must be protected from such knowledge as effectively as possible. Such a conclusion has usually been reached, partly because relatives fear the patient's reaction to knowledge about dying, partly because they prefer to 'bracket' this recognition themselves, and partly because they are surrounded by people who assume that this is the only tenable view to hold. In a hazy way relatives are aware of the conflict between any possibility of rewarding social interaction and withholding the truth. They sense that any mutually constructed and shared reality is not viable when they are constrained by secret knowledge and fear of disclosure. I found that this was a significant problem for the relatives of dying people because they had reached a position which seemed clear enough, but which they recognised as potentially destructive and difficult to maintain. The social worker should acknowledge the confusing nature of this dilemma and relatives' feelings that it is less painful to ignore the reality of impending loss. However, it often comes as a relief for relatives to hear that, as they rightly guess, the solution to the dilemma is not as simple as others have suggested. From knowledge and experience, the social worker can point out that many patients come to know that they are dying and that they may want to share this knowledge with people who are important to them. It should be explained that as long as relatives are open to this possibility, do not jump in with cheerful denials as soon as the subject is raised, and allow the patient to take the initiative, they will not cause any harm or distress. By removing the *assumption* that it is better to lie and to avoid the possibility that the patient will not recover, relatives are given the confidence to listen to the patient's cues and to respond on the basis of what he 'tells' them through verbal and non-verbal communication. It sometimes requires a simple reminder that relatives are likely to know the patient better than anyone else and to recognise when he is worried or withdrawn. This gives them the necessary sense of their own ability to respond appropriately. The social worker can thus help relatives to grasp the elements of their confusion in relation to this problem by explaining what we know about dying people and their reactions, and provide encouragement and reassurance that they will be able to handle interaction without causing the patient distress. Relatives should be warned that just as they will sometimes need to 'bracket' their anticipation of loss in order to go on living, the patient may also need to do this. If the patient sometimes speaks or acts as though there is nothing wrong, this does not mean he wishes to reject their help or push them away, but that for the time being his awareness of dying must be moved to one side. Since this is a complex area, relatives will probably want to discuss it at various times during a terminal illness. The aim of the initial discussion is to 'free' relatives from the assumption that they will protect the patient by refusing to acknowledge his terminal condition, and to help them understand their own and the patient's reactions to impending loss.

Close relatives will often be confused about what they should tell other family members, especially children. Some of their concern will be related to protecting the patient from knowledge of his terminal condition, and this should have been explored by the social worker. Relatives will usually have a good idea of those friends and family members who are likely to be helpful and those who will be embarrassed, avoid subsequent contact with the patient, or think that they know all the right answers. It should be clear that members of the immediate family need to be told the exact state of affairs, and the disclosure of information to others needs to be based on knowledge of their likely reactions. The terminal period will obviously be extremely difficult, and if a husband or wife has a good friend whom they consider supportive they should not feel guilty about discussing the problem with them. The immediate reaction of many people is that children should be protected from the truth. However, children are quick to pick up signs of tension and inconsistent information, and imagined possibilities can be more frightening and unpredictable than knowledge about what is actually the case. If this area is discussed with relatives they can be helped to anticipate these difficulties and to work out ways of giving truthful information which is compatible with the maintenance of hope. For example, a child might be told that 'Daddy is very ill'; and in answer to the question 'Will he die?' that 'I don't know if the doctors will be able to make him better, but they are trying their best.' If parents have thought about the question in advance and had the opportunity to discuss their worries in this context, they are less likely to be angry or confused or to blurt out inappropriate answers. In essence the social worker should help relatives to define and focus on a problem and to consider the implications of tackling it in various ways. This is a vital task, since other professional workers and well-intentioned friends may advise relatives on the basis of their own uncompromising assumptions about the 'best way' to do things. If relatives have not been given the opportunity to explore their own feelings and to think about what the situation means to them, the dying patient, and significant others, they will be ill-prepared to manage important areas of inter-action. In this case relationships may become distorted, individuals socially isolated, and a sense of control and self-esteem attenuated.

Through guiding the definition of problem areas and enabling the constructive discussion of specific anxieties and questions, the social worker has already helped relatives to regain some sense of control and self-esteem. Rather than seeing themselves as victims of a cruel fate, they can begin to work out their own contribution to managing the terminal phase in a positive way. It is possible for them to appreciate that their relationship with the terminally ill person does not have to hang in limbo for the remaining time which they have together, but can be developed and enjoyed. There will be difficulties as time goes on. Relatives will become physically tired, will not always be able to respond in an appropriate and considered way, and will feel angry about the seeming futility of all their efforts. The patient too, may express anger or become depressed, will make excessive demands and will sometimes fail to understand the feelings of others. The social worker should be available throughout this period in order to help relatives clarify conflicting feelings about their own reactions and those of others. If relatives have regular opportunities to reassess the problem, to discuss new areas of strain, and to test out their ideas about managing the situa-tion, their sense of control may be confirmed and reinforced. A social worker can never do the work for a client, but can help the client to make a start by translating what is per-ceived as an overwhelming problem into manageable parts, each of which may be understood and tackled in a relatively well-defined and limited way.

During the terminal phase, the social worker may also have to act as an advocate and mediator in relation to other services. The general practitioner and community nursing services may not be aware of particular problems and rela-tives may be diffident about asking for help. It may be neces-sary to apply for financial help for increased heating or a special diet. Arranging for someone to sit with the patient will enable a tired and worried husband or wife to go out for an evening or get a good night's sleep. These may appear to be small points. If however, people are pushed to the limit, attention to such details may make a disproportionate difference to their ability to manage the terminal phase successfully and this in turn will significantly influence their sense of control and self-esteem.

Working with the family

It has been noted that difficulties for the whole family are likely to revolve around communication breakdown, social isolation of members, redistribution of roles, and personal confusion. The uncertainty and conflicting demands of the terminal phase are likely to put particular pressures on family relationships and functioning. Family members are unlikely to resolve these difficulties if, in the first instance, they have unclear or inadequate information about diagnosis and prognosis. It is vital that the whole family should have an opportunity to discuss and clarify the nature of the illness, and its course as far as can be predicted. They may need the social worker to help them formulate their questions, to put them to the doctor in such a way that they receive adequate answers, or to interpret the use of medical terms. Wherever possible, all members of the immediate family should be included in discussing plans for looking after the patient at home so that individual and joint concerns can be expressed and worked out. The social worker can anticipate situations where an adolescent daughter might be asked to stay in one night to look after the patient, so that another member of the family can have time off to visit friends. If the whole family have not participated in the initial planning, limitations imposed on outside activities or bringing friends home can be viewed with resentment. Such feelings may be directed towards the patient engendering further reactions of anger and guilt .

Difficulties in communication may arise because the normal network of interaction has been disrupted, for example by terminal illness of a mother. I have already discussed ways of helping both patient and relatives to understand the social distance which may result from different perceptions of real-

ity. Often the social worker must act as interpreter and mediator, explaining what individuals know, why they may be
angry or withdrawn, how they perceive their own situation
and the actions of others. In this way she can help the family
develop an area of shared understanding as a basis for continuing interaction. This is an important task when people
may be involved in attempts to protect each other from
potentially distressing information to the detriment of open
and spontaneous communication. If the social worker also
understands that the patient is responding in a normal way to
knowledge that he is dying, by for example withdrawing his
investment in social exchanges, this can be explained to other
members of the family who may be making unrealistic demands on the assumption that they are being rejected and
abandoned. Time spent explaining how the patient may behave and anticipating the reactions of other family members
will help to prevent a later spiral of misunderstandings,
recriminations and guilt. It is not always easy to modify
responses on the basis of knowledge. The social worker may
have to go over the same explanation on several occasions,
helping the family to sort out what they can realistically
expect of themselves and the patient during the terminal stage.
It may sometimes be necessary for the social worker to
acknowledge that the demands of living with someone who
is dying are bound to make people feel angry, guilty, frustrated, impatient, and so on.

Enabling the shared expression of feelings among family
members is an important task during this time. The family
are likely to feel restrained from showing that they are angry
or sad about what is happening, fearing that they have no
right to do so, and that they will further distress themselves,
others, and the patient. Personal pain may lead to social
isolation and the breakdown of communication. The social
worker may enable family members to express these feelings
by acknowledging that they exist, making direct statements
to the effect that someone looks tense, angry, or sad, saying
that many people feel like this and that it is legitimate both
to have such feelings and to talk about them. It is often the
case that a family are only able to express their feelings when
there is someone available to provide an element of safety

and control which they fear they may lose. The social worker should represent this assurance of stability through a firm and confident approach which cannot be ruffled in the face of anger and pain. The worker may feel ruffled, but she must be perceived as reliable and trustworthy in a situation which threatens to be overwhelming. If the worker is also seen as tolerant and concerned, the family will be able to talk about those painful areas of their experience which are difficult to discuss in other situations, where people may be embarrassed, alarmed and take action to terminate the conversation. In essence then, the social worker must be able to act in a way which cannot be *expected* of friends, neighbours or members of the extended family, and to provide that thread of continuity and stability which is so precarious for those who are struggling with the disruption of their reality. In the next chapter, I will move on to consider the final breakdown of reality when death occurs and the habitual form of social interaction and confirmation of identity can no longer be maintained.

7
Bereavement

For man's greatness does not reside merely in the destiny
of the species; each individual is an empire. When a
mine caves in and closes over the head of a single miner,
the life of the community is suspended.

Antoine de Saint-Exupery, *Wind, Sand and Stars* (1939)

The nature of grief reactions following bereavement are by
now well documented, and as I have shown, have been discussed and explained from a number of theoretical and therapeutic viewpoints. Research initiatives have been able to
identify some individuals and groups who may be particularly
vulnerable when faced with the death of a significant other,
and to outline those responses which may or may not facilitate recovery from the impact of loss. The observation that
bereavement engenders acute distress, social and emotional
disorganisation, and the possibility of longer-term debilita-
tion, has led to a consideration of whether professional
intervention should be provided in this context. Some attempts have been made to evaluate the degree of successful
recovery where professional help has been made available
to the bereaved, as compared to those who have not been
offered similar assistance. Polak *et al.* (1973) and Kincey
(1974) found no difference between those people who received help, and a control group who did not, in relation to
their adjustment several months after bereavement. However,
work by Gerber *et al.* (1975) and Raphael (1977) has demonstrated that appropriate help given at the time of bereavement,

and for as long as necessary following this, does facilitate a better outcome for many people than is the case for those who do not receive such help. Parkes (1977) also reports encouraging results from his study of an 'aftercare service' provided for the bereaved and developed by St Christopher's Hospice in London. Research which attempts to establish the relationship between successful adjustment to bereavement and the offer of professional help is open to the same kinds of methodological problems which are involved in any evaluative exercise of this type, and which have made it difficult to reach any accurate assessment of social work intervention. Perhaps the most evident reason for encouraging social workers to develop their skills in working with the bereaved, is that we know the experience of loss is painful and overwhelming, that appropriate help is not always available from usual social networks, and that personal and social resources are sometimes insufficient to enable a successful resolution of mourning. We also know a great deal about what needs to be done if the bereaved individual and family are not to remain incapacitated by loss and immobilised by grief. While it is important to evaluate and to revise knowledge and methods of working, we cannot wait for the legitimation of research before confronting the distress of those who are bereaved.

I have suggested in Chapter 4 that bereavement must be viewed as a social as well as an intra-psychic experience, and that the process of recovery must also be seen in terms of social interaction, meaning and the construction of a new reality. The impact of loss may be understood as occurring at three levels. First, the taken-for-granted reality which forms the basis for all our routine actions, conversations, and expectations, has suddenly fallen apart. Chaos has permeated what once went unquestioned as a stable and repetitive way of life, carried on in the context of shared and accumulated knowledge about the past and expectations about the future. A world which was formerly taken for granted as being reliable and orderly has become chaotic and potentially dangerous. Not only has reality as formerly understood become disrupted, but the very people who could previously be relied upon to engage in normal social interaction now appear to be confused about appropriate behaviour, are lost for words, or simply withdraw in embarrassed silence. It is not surprising that the bereaved express feelings of lack of control and direction, and anxieties about impending danger or being in a 'hostile world'. The world *has* ceased to be reliable and trustworthy. It has become a place in which anything could happen, and other people often do little to alleviate this sense of uncertainty and insecurity.

Second, if the bereaved individual has lost a person who was significant in day-to-day interaction and the shared construction of reality, he is likely to experience an attenuation of meaning. All those actions and conversations which were carried out in interaction with the lost person and which derived their meaning from mutual understanding of past experience, present purpose, and future plans, now cease to be relevant. Reality, as constructed and shared with a significant other, fails to have any meaning when the partner no longer exists. The observation that bereaved individuals continue to act as though the lost person were still alive, is consistent with this interpretation. Laying the table for two, expecting a dead husband to return from work at the usual time, seeing and talking to the lost person, represent a continuation of habitual actions and expectations which cannot be abandoned at the drop of a hat. Furthermore, these actions continue to have meaning until the reality of loss is fully grasped and accepted. Such behaviour does not necessarily indicate that the person who is left is searching for and finding the lost individual in an instinctive response, but that reality and meaning cannot be immediately relinquished in the short term. Gradually, it becomes clear that the partner to this interaction is no longer available and the expected responses no longer forthcoming. Once this is recognised, reality disintegrates and the bereaved describe their feelings in terms of despair and meaninglessness. There can be no meaning or purpose to everyday life if this is not confirmed and validated through interaction with the significant other.

Third, it is only through social interaction that a sense of the individual's place in the world, and his identity, can be maintained. An awareness of the 'I' and 'Me' elements of the self, referred to earlier, can only be grasped in relation to others as they present and confirm identity through inter-action. The greatest distress and confusion will obviously result from the loss of a significant person who has confirmed the other's identity through continuing social exchanges. We may regret the death of someone who lived down the road or a distant relative and may be concerned for those who will mourn the loss, but our own social world and our identity within it remain secure and protected from disruption. It is in this sense that it is possible to understand the remarks of bereaved people when they say that they have lost some essential part of themselves, that they feel empty or hollow, or that they feel strange and unreal.

In summary, loss imposes a disruption of taken-for-granted reality, an attenuation of meaning, and a threat to identity. The initial reactions of shock, disbelief, hearing and seeing the dead person, and subsequent feelings of anger, disorganisa-tion and meaninglessness can be readily understood within this framework. There may be particular responses to loss, depending on the status of the deceased as a partner in social interaction. The death of a husband or wife is likely to high-light the whole range of difficulties associated with the disruption of meaning and identity. The death of a child may raise greater, more profound anxieties about reality and meaning than about personal identity, where significant others are still available to confirm this through social interaction. The death of a parent may disrupt those channels of com-munication and patterns of interaction which provide any sense of stability and enable the development and confirma-tion of identity and self-esteem. Thus, in order to understand the particular impact of loss, it is necessary to appreciate the part played by the deceased in one or more areas of reality construction, meaning and confirmation of identity. The extent to which the maintenance of reality, meaning and identity breaks down following bereavement will depend on the significance of the dead person's former contribution, the ability of survivors to reallocate responsibilities in these areas, and the availability of alternative resources. It has been noted that such reorganisation of tasks in relation to a continuing need for the confirmation of reality and identity may impose particular strains on the bereaved. For example, a widow may impose inappropriate expectations on her son, or bereaved parents may put pressure on remaining children to take over the affective functions of a dead sibling. Whatever the relationship of the bereaved to the deceased, there appears to be general agreement that any successful adjustment to loss can only be accomplished if those who are left carry out what has been termed their 'grief-work'.

The idea of *work* is relevant because adjustment to bereavement involves considerable pain and effort in recognising the reality of loss, accepting that the lost person is no longer available, and seeking alternative relationships and avenues for rewarding social interaction. In essence, grief-work demands a disengagement from the relationship and interaction with the deceased, so freeing the bereaved to develop relationships elsewhere. If the bereaved cannot tolerate the pain which is associated with recognising and accepting the reality of loss, or the sense of meaninglessness and attenuation of identity which follow, they may avoid or distort reality in such a way that grief-work does not occur. Inhibited or delayed mourning may reflect an inability to recognise the reality of loss, while prolonged or extreme mourning may illustrate an unwillingness to accept the finality of loss and the disengagement and disruption which this requires. For those whose expressions of grief are blocked or discouraged by others, who do not have time to grieve because of other demands, or who can not give up their relationship with the deceased because of 'unfinished business', an already insecure sense of identity and self-esteem, or a dearth of alternative avenues for social interaction, grief-work may be avoided or overlooked. If this happens it is likely that disengagement from the deceased will not be fully accomplished. The ability to develop new relationships, and to engage in the social construction of a reality which recognises the absence of the lost person, will be difficult to attain. Since the bereaved person's sense of identity and confirmation of self-esteem will still be very much tied to their relationship with the deceased, they may be vulnerable to the impact of future crises or experiences of loss. The inability to find new ways of exerting control and defining purposes in relation to everyday life and social interaction, will further exacerbate the potentially over-whelming nature of future problems. There are thus good reasons why the bereaved should be helped to confront the task of grief-work and the process of carrying this out. Many people with adequate personal and social resources will be able to recognise the reality of loss, express their grief, and face the confusion and disruption of their social world. However, for the reasons mentioned above, some will avoid or side-step this painful and confusing process. By doing so they may inhibit the development of new relationships through which the confirmation of identity and control and the construction of a modified reality and meaning, may be accomplished.

It is possible to identify several tasks which should be undertaken during the course of mourning and adjustment to a world in which the deceased no longer exists. These are first, recognising the reality of loss; second, accepting the reality of loss; third, disengaging from the deceased; fourth, facing the disruption of reality and meaning; fifth, making new relationships and constructing new meanings. Raphael (1980) has suggested that the principal aims of those who seek to help the bereaved can be simply outlined. They are: to offer 'basic human comfort and support'; to encourage the expression of grief with reference to the particular needs and situation of the individual concerned; to promote the mourning process; and to accept that where possible the activity of mourning should be accommodated by significant members of the family and social network. The notion that social workers should 'help' people to do certain things is commonly accepted. In the following pages I will consider more precisely how social workers may help the bereaved to begin and accomplish their grief-work, and to achieve the principal aims of effective intervention in this context.

Recognising the reality of loss

As we know, it is common for the newly bereaved to be shocked and numbed by news of a death. In the first few days or weeks, they may also be aware of the presence of the deceased and engage in many aspects of their habitual interaction: carrying on conversations, seeing the deceased coming in or sitting in a favourite chair, and making plans which take the participation of the dead person for granted. The full impact of their loss will not yet be felt. During this time the bereaved are likely to be well supported by relatives and close friends who may help to carry out the practical arrangements surrounding death and involving registration, immediate financial concerns, and organising the funeral. Because the newly bereaved tend to be protected and organised by others there is little opportunity to face or experience the reality of loss. At this time reality and the question of meaning are suspended while everything happens around the bereaved. They continue the routine activities of everyday life but without meaning bestowed by engaging and being engaged by others. The activity, the arrangements, the funeral, the concern of relatives and friends, establish that someone has died but this may be perceived as unreal and distanced from the personal experience of the bereaved. It might almost have happened to someone else.

Gradually, the nature of others' reactions, the communication of sympathy and condolences, participation in the funeral, and a growing awareness that the deceased is no longer available, confirm and reinforce the reality of loss. The death may be recognised but not yet accepted. Any social worker in contact with the newly bereaved should allow the initial period of numbness without attempting any active work towards the recognition of loss. It is at this time that the worker may help with practical issues, and be available to encourage recognition and acceptance when the truth can no longer be avoided. As the bereaved begin to experience the absence of the deceased, the social worker can help in several ways. First, the bereaved may be angry with the dead for leaving them, with others who cannot fill the space and who do not comprehend the enormity of loss, with God for allowing this to happen, with the world for falling apart, and with themselves for the things they have left undone and the things which can never be undone. While relatives and friends expect and accept distress and sadness, they may well withdraw from the expression of anger which they cannot understand and which they perceive as unjustified in the light of all their attempts to help. The social worker can tolerate this anger, tell the bereaved through her attitude and words that their feelings are natural and acceptable, and provide the reassurance that someone is there who will neither lose control nor withdraw if the going gets rough. Some of this anger must simply be expressed. It can not be redirected or explained away, but sharing it with someone who is not shocked or alarmed can demonstrate that the bereaved are not bad, different, frightening or destructive because they feel in this way. Anger which the bereaved may direct against themselves for real or imagined failings in their relationships with the deceased, must be recognised as a valid area of concern. Friendly remarks like, 'Don't be silly, you did all you could', or 'There's no point in torturing yourself like this', or 'You must forget all those upsetting things', are intended to be reassuring and helpful. Their effect, however, is to deny the importance of these feelings for the bereaved and to minimise the significance of relationships with the deceased. The social worker can accept that people will feel angry because they have failed in certain respects, while pointing out that there are certain things which could not have been anticipated or changed and for which the bereaved are unjustly blaming themselves. By accepting the validity of some self-directed anger, the social worker is also in a better position to challenge unwarranted or unrealistic expectations which give rise to self-blame. The bereaved can be helped to express their anger, to sort out where it is valid and where is is not, and to develop some perspective which clarifies and orders their mass of intense and confused feelings. There may always be regret about the imperfections in a relationship, or the impatience and misunderstandings which caused the deceased to be distressed when he most needed comfort and love. However, the shift from anger and self-blame to sadness and regret, can only be accomplished through an acceptance by self and others of the reality of these feelings and the capacity for failure and competence shown by all human beings in their social relationships.

Second, the social worker can encourage the developing recognition of loss by avoiding retreat or denial. Friends might greet the bereaved with 'I don't know what to say'' or 'I'm sorry to hear about your loss'. As Steele (1977) has suggested, the first statement may really mean 'I'm afraid' because there is nothing which I or anyone else can do to resolve the problem, the whole issue is too big to handle in a few words, and a direct contemplation of total disruption is too personally daunting for concrete expression. The second statement avoids mention of the finality of death. Loss does not sound too bad, and rather implies that something has been mislaid and may yet be found.

The social worker cannot afford to show that she is afraid, and must avoid maintaining distance from the bereaved by making formal and empty statements. Instead, she should say something to the effect that 'I'm sorry to hear your husband has died. I know that nothing I can say at the moment will make you feel better but I want you to know that I am here to help in any way I can'. The simple rule is to refer to the deceased as being *dead*, in terms of direct reference to what has happened, the use of appropriate tense, and a response to remarks like, 'I still can't believe it', or 'It hasn't really sunk in', which confirms reality rather than merely accepting the avoidance of 'not believing' or 'not grasping' the truth. This may sound brutal, but it is directed at encouraging a growing recognition which cannot be rendered less painful by pretending that loss can somehow be absorbed and accommodated while avoiding explicit awareness. The social worker must consistently erode any false protection offered by denial. This means facing the bereaved with the finality of death through conversation about the deceased as having died, rather than 'gone missing', and as having no reference point in the present or future tense. This process is not intended to be brutal or uncaring, but gently corrective as the worker uncompromisingly responds in a way which confirms rather than avoids the reality of total and final loss. The social worker must reinforce cues which gradually compel a recognition that death has occurred.

Accepting the reality of loss and disengagement from the deceased

Grief-work can only proceed if the recognition of death is

accompanied by an acceptance of loss. It is possible, for any of the reasons mentioned earlier, for the bereaved to recognise that a death has occurred but to avoid accepting that the deceased is no longer available for continuing interaction and confirmation of their identity. Attempts to keep everything as before, to prepare the deceased person's favourite meals, to keep all his clothes and personal belongings, to take over his hobbies, may be a source of comfort if the bereaved are able to accept, at the same time, that these measures provide a temporary respite from 'going it alone'. If, however, they fail to demonstrate an acceptance that the deceased is absent and an awareness of their own aloneness, these activities may indicate their refusal to grasp that death is final and everything has changed. Continuing and extreme feelings of guilt, and the need for forgiveness, may point to a breakdown in personal identity, the inability to recognise and accept their own mistakes and imperfections, and a strong dependence on the deceased for any confirmation of self-esteem. If the bereaved appear not to be accepting the reality of loss, it may be the case that they came to their relationship with the deceased without much sense of their own individuality and self-worth, and that their contribution to the construction of a shared reality was therefore marginal. In such a situation, it might be appropriate to refer the bereaved for psychiatric help or the social worker may have to undertake a long period of work aimed at understanding and correcting a poorly developed sense of identity, feelings of low self-esteem, and a negative self-image.

The bereaved will begin to show their acceptance of loss when they talk about the deceased in terms of death and their own aloneness. They may comment, for example: 'I am only just beginning to grasp the fact that he is dead'; or 'The house seems so empty'; or 'Everything has just come crashing down around my ears.' When loss becomes real in this way, the pain of being alone and facing each day without the deceased begins to be felt and expressed. Once again, the social worker can help in several ways. First, the worker should continue to encourage the recognition and acceptance that the deceased is in fact dead, and lost to our world of everyday interaction and meaning. Second, the worker can

tolerate the pain and sorrow which this involves and maintain an attitude of concern and willingness to be *with* the
bereaved. This may sound like doing nothing in particular.
As I have suggested in previous chapters, however, expressing
an attitude of concern is a very active business and requires
considerable self-knowledge about one's own reactions to
death, bereavement, personal loss and our own (and others')
mortality. It also requires consideration of our own 'presentation of self' and the way in which we are perceived by
others. It is also important that the social worker is able to
encourage a developing acceptance of loss and enable the
expression of sorrow because such help may not be available
from other sources. Jones (1977) has commented that once
the activities of arranging the funeral and supporting the
newly bereaved are over, informal support systems tend to
be withdrawn. The bereaved may thus be left without effective help at this time or may be faced with well-intentioned
but inappropriate comments like: 'You will soon feel better';
or 'Things won't seem so bad in a few weeks.' Things are as bad
as they possibly could be, and any attempt to avoid this fact
serves to minimise the significance and reality of loss and to
increase social distance and isolation. The social worker's
task is thus to enhance opportunities for recognising and
accepting the finality of loss, and enabling the feeling and
expression of pain and sorrow. Any natural and spontaneous
wish to provide comfort by reference to a 'better time' in the
future, at the expense of facing the pain of the present, can
only hinder the progress of grief-work. A social worker who
makes such comments may also be viewed as untrustworthy
in the sense of withdrawing from social engagement and the
sharing of sorrow. We have to recognise that there can be
little comfort when the bereaved face tomorrow and every
other day without the deceased. What the social worker can
provide is some sense of stability, continuity, and reliability
in a world which has ceased to have any meaning or purpose.
It is only in this way that any sense of comfort can be conveyed and accepted.

Third, the process of accepting the reality of loss and
disengaging from the deceased, requires that the meaning of
relationships and shared reality should be reviewed and placed

in an appropriate historical perspective. The bereaved will want to talk about their lives with the deceased, and while doing so will continue the work of confirming that these things happened in the past *before* their loved ones *died*. Facilitating this conversation may be accomplished in several ways. Through being available, attentive, interested, and responsive, the social worker can convey that she wants to hear about this topic and that it is legitimate to talk about it. Once again, the communication of this message is important. Relatives and friends may be willing to listen for so long, but the bereaved person's need to go over past experiences and shared activities on many occasions may lead them to say; 'You shouldn't be dwelling on the past so much'; or 'It's morbid to keep going over the same things'; or 'You should be thinking of the future now.' They may show by subtle cues that they are impatient or embarrassed, or avoid interaction with the bereaved altogether. Corazzini (1980) suggests that enabling the bereaved to talk about their lives with the deceased may be accomplished by means of looking at photographs, referring to family momentoes, asking about interesting pictures or ornaments, or joint hobbies, all of which will be connected with shared experiences and activities. The social worker should thus not only convey that she is open and prepared to listen, but actively participate by providing stimuli 'that will help the bereaved to tell the most complete story of the deceased' (Corazzini, 1980, p. 77) and, I would add, of their life together.

The object of this exercise is to help the bereaved describe what their lives were like before their loss, and to clarify the boundary between this and the new and different situation which they now have to face. The conversation clearly places their relationship and experiences with the deceased in the past. There are two further advantages of talking in this way. The first is that the bereaved may remember the good and rewarding aspects of their relationship with the deceased, and this may be a source of present and future support and a confirmation that something worthwhile has been achieved. This also serves to reinforce feelings of self-esteem and to ameliorate the attitude of hostility and anger which may influence interaction with relatives and friends. Second, if the bereaved have had a particularly ambivalent or problematic relationship with the deceased, they may be feeling angry about what they perceive as wasted time, have a poor sense of self-esteem, and blame themselves for real and imagined faults. While helpful listeners may consider it to be a 'healthy' sign if the bereaved talk positively about the deceased, they may be less ready to listen to the expression of anger and self-blame. Attempts may be made to avoid the discussion of such painful topics or to take a firm line with the bereaved who 'speak ill of the dead' or dwell on upsetting aspects of the past. It is also difficult for the bereaved to consider negative elements of a relationship with relatives and friends, since the latter may wish to preserve their own image of the deceased and to forget difficulties or conflicts about which they feel nothing can be done. Fear of being perceived as disloyal or alienating friends and relatives may also inhibit the bereaved from expressing any angry feelings towards the deceased. Allowing the bereaved to talk about the distressing aspects of their relationship with the deceased may avoid the possibility that anger and self-blame will become the focus of their feelings about themselves and others, thus leading to further isolation and diminishing self-esteem. The social worker can also help the bereaved to clarify the difference between real areas of conflict and their part in promoting these, and what they may unrealistically come to view as being totally their fault. Any attempt to convince the bereaved that they had no part in causing or reinforcing conflict, is unhelpful. What is required, is that the bereaved are able to develop a balance between totally blaming the deceased or totally blaming themselves, and to reach a compromise which recognises the good and bad parts of a relationship and normal human frailty. In this way they can work out a memory of the deceased as a person, rather than as a victim on one hand, or a persecutor on the other.

Because the social worker is prepared to listen when others are not, to stimulate discussion about the deceased when others consider this to be 'morbid', and to encourage the expression of negative as well as positive feelings, it is likely that the bereaved will be able to recognise and accept their loss. The deceased are not forgotten, but they become located in the past while their memory is incorporated into present reality. Through the process of grief-work, the deceased may thus be placed in historical and emotional perspective.

Facing disruption and making new relationships

Once the bereaved begin to accept the reality of loss, they will face the meaninglessness and purposelessness so often observed and recorded by researchers and practitioners. There is now no comfort to be gained through initial numbness or continuing habitual patterns of interaction. Every detail of joint activities carried out by husband and wife, or parents and children, ceases to have meaning and a radical change in daily routines must be accommodated. Taken-for-granted reality has shattered, the world has become an untrustworthy place, the confirmation of personal identity has been disrupted, and relationships with others now have to be re-established on a completely different basis.

This may be the most difficult period for the bereaved and for the social worker. For the bereaved, because they have 'given up' the deceased and have nothing to replace their lost relationships and sense of purpose; and for the social worker, because she has worked hard at encouraging an acceptance of loss, only apparently to lead the bereaved to acute sadness and sometimes despair. It may be at this time that the social worker feels most useless and most unsure about what should be done. The social worker can, however, do several things. First, the worker can be reliable and trustworthy as mentioned before. This is particularly important when life has come to be viewed as unreliable and unstable, and when friends and sometimes relatives have begun to withdraw or to be at a loss as to how to help. Second, the social worker can be patient and refuse to break off contact or to be overwhelmed by the seeming hopelessness of the situation. Third, the social worker can act, for a short time, as a partner in social interaction in order to confirm the bereaved person's sense of identity and self-esteem. This involves accepting feelings as valid, and avoiding the tem-tation to say 'Snap out of it', or 'You are lucky compared to some people', or 'Everyone else copes with this kind of thing.' It also means accepting the bereaved as individuals and not as a category who are frightening or difficult to approach. By engaging the bereaved in social interaction and 'playing back' to them that they are not unusual, they will be able to regain a sense of self in relation to the social worker as a 'significant other'. It is important to recognise here that the social worker should act as a 'bridge' or a temporary 'stand in' until the bereaved regain sufficient confidence to open up interaction with other people. The worker should not become the most important person or the only person who can be relied upon to provide stability and continuity in the long term. As Raphael (1980, p. 161) points out, 'bereavement counselling has well defined goals. One of these is *not* to become a replacement for the person who has died.'

One of the ways in which the social worker can avoid becoming a replacement is to be alert to the progress made by the bereaved. Gradually, and with prompting and support from the worker, the bereaved will begin to wonder if they can renew old relationships and make new ones. They may wonder what people will think if they return to work or whether it will be considered improper for them to go alone, or with a friend, to some social occasion. Part of their difficulty concerns how *they* will cope with the queries, embarrassment, or solicitude of others, and the worker can help them to anticipate this and to prepare appropriate responses. A further problem which worries the bereaved is how they will manage social interaction now that they are single as opposed to one of a couple, or a mother or father who has lost a child. The worker can help by understanding these problems as being natural, by anticipating with the bereaved what may happen and how they may react, and by providing encouragement and firm reassurance about their ability to manage social interaction. The worker can also help the bereaved to sort out what will be best for them, and to support them in carrying this out in situations where others may be suggesting that they are not ready to go back to work, that they should be more aware of their status as newly bereaved widows, that they should move house, take a holiday, concentrate on the children, and so on. After each tentative step, the bereaved will gain in confidence, will learn new ways of handling interaction, and will develop relationships on a new and realistic basis. There may well be disappointments and setbacks, and the social worker should be available to assess the nature of apparent difficulties, to discuss methods of coping with them, and to reassure the bereaved that learning new roles and regaining a sense of personal identity must be a gradual and is often a daunting business. When a task has been successfully accomplished the social worker should grasp the opportunity to reinforce self-esteem, and to provide further encouragement for the bereaved to take the next step.

Throughout this process there may be practical problems concerning finances, housing, caring for children and so on. Initially, the social worker may take a positive and direct role in liaising with other agencies and sorting out practical difficulties. However, in order to help the bereaved regain their own self-confidence and sense of control over their social world, it becomes necessary to help them take direct action, albeit with advice or relevant information provided by the social worker. Working out a plan of action with the bereaved and encouraging them to follow this through may provide the first opportunity for reinforcement of self-confidence. From this point it becomes progressively easier to handle other problems and develop appropriate solutions.

Sometimes the bereaved will face particular problems, about which everyone is keen to give usually conflicting advice. One such difficulty is what to tell children about the death of a parent. In such a situation, the social worker should ask the bereaved what they think about this. Whatever their response, they should be encouraged to think through the implications of any course of action. This involves planning what they will say and anticipating any repercussions and methods of dealing with these. A remaining parent who says it seems kinder to tell the children that their mother or father has 'gone away for a while', or has gone to a wonderful place called Heaven, can be asked gently what they will say when the children ask why she or he has not returned. Or how they will respond to the query that Heaven cannot be such a wonderful place if everyone else is so upset about the departure. Parents may need to discuss a child's need to continually confirm and clarify what has happened, and the importance of being consistent and honest in their answers. They may wish to consider how to handle children's questions about what happens when people die. Where do they go? Do they breath? Do they eat? How can they live in the ground? Will they ever come back? Don't they love the family any more? Concern may also be expressed about taking children to funerals and parents may encounter pressure not to do so. However, children as well as adults must come to grasp the finality of death and the reality of loss. This will not be achieved if they are protected by well-meaning parents. Schiff (1977, p. 4) remarks in this connection, 'I would not allow my son, aged twelve, to view the body of his dead brother, because of the horror I felt seeing it. Unfortunately, no one told me I would harm my son with my protectiveness. And harm him it did because it took many years for him to lay his brother's ghost to rest.' She also comments that her daughter, then aged 4, had an even less realistic grasp of her brother's death because she was not allowed to attend his funeral and that 'she is resentful even after all these years that she was cheated of the experience'. The social worker's role is not to tell the bereaved how to handle such matters, but to give them the opportunity of anticipating and trying out various approaches to the problem with someone who can guide and focus discussion rather than telling them what is right or wrong.

Work with families will take largely the same form as that described for families who have a terminally ill member. Enabling the expression of feelings, acting as a communication link where individuals are in danger of becoming isolated, guiding the clarification of problems and consideration of solutions, can sometimes be more readily achieved by some-one who is outside the immediate family circle. I came across a case where a 14-year-old boy had been on holiday with friends when his mother died after a terminal illness. He had been told of the death by an adult in the party and although saddened was advised to continue his holiday. By the time he returned, the funeral service had been held and the rest of the family were handling their grief as relatively isolated individuals. The boy came back to a household where no one shared their feelings and no one talked about what had happened. It was as though he had imagined the whole thing. Finding no way of expressing his own grief or gaining comfort from those around him, he became progressively more angry, unwilling to comply with task allocations, and withdrawn from others. The social worker's task was first, to help the other family members recognise how the situation was viewed by the boy and how they were all coping with their grief. And second, to ask them what they felt could be done about this. Talking about grief and pain, and acknowledging a fear of sharing strong feelings, is often sufficient to allow the expression of anger, guilt, sadness, and so on. The social worker can identify such feelings, encourage their expression, and provide some sense of safety and control which may have previously been absent. Where it becomes apparent that family members do not *trust* each other to offer comfort and understanding and are therefore unwilling to show their vulnerability, the social worker may need to help them consider the nature of relationships within the family and the way in which these fears have developed. In this above case, the family were able to talk about their feelings and to include the boy in this. They also agreed to go with him to the grave so that he could locate and grasp the reality of what had happened. I have met many older children and adults who feel resentful that they were excluded from the opportunity to attend a funeral or visit a grave, because it was considered that this would be too distressing for them. What it did achieve was to leave them confused about the meaning of death, and shut off from an explanation of others' sorrow, the frightening reasons for which they could only imagine.

Using community resources

There is a danger that social workers may fail to consider the relevance of help beyond the professional knowledge and experience which they can contribute. Such professional short-sightedness neglects the possibility that clients may view other sources of help as being equally valid and acceptable, if not more so. In the field of adoption, it is clear that prospective adopters see other adoptive parents as providing advice and support which may be less acceptable from social workers (see Middlestadt, 1978 Smith, 1980). It has been noted that social workers should not replace the usual support networks if these are able to meet the needs of the bereaved. Similarly, it may be the case that other bereaved people can understand the feelings and respond to the grief of the newly bereaved, in a way which is both appropriate and acceptable to those who need help.

Silverman (1970) reports on a programme where women who had been widowed about three years previously, were recruited to work with the recently widowed. The widow 'caregivers' had all become involved in community activities following their husbands' deaths, and it was through contact with community organisations that they were recruited. The advantages of the scheme are seen as being first, that widow caregivers are perceived as able to *understand* the conflicting feelings of pride, the wish for independence, and the sorrow and confusion, rather than just offering sympathy. Second, the recently widowed are released from the constraints of worrying about how the helpers will react or whether they will be embarrassed and uncertain. Third, the widow caregivers can at the same time accept the normality of grief and its associated feelings, while showing by their presence as helpers that life can have meaning and purpose later on. Fourth, they can offer direct advice which may be more acceptable because of their 'privileged status' and can provide encouragement to the recently widowed in order to help them develop new relationships and new interests. The opportunity to discuss problems and ways of helping is built into the scheme through weekly meetings between the widow caregivers as a group, and an outside consultant. Schiff (1977) believes the death of a child has such a devastating impact on parents and siblings, that she has written about her own experience of bereavement in an effort to help others who have suffered a similar loss. While she recognises that professional intervention may sometimes be necessary and helpful, she argues that those who are bereaved can often gain more comfort, understanding and hope from other people who have also been through the despair and recovery which follow loss. She says of her and her husband's attempts to help other bereaved parents that, 'what we had was something few could give them. We had experience. When they saw us, they saw a mother and father with a dead child who were able to cope.'

The work of the caregivers, like that of a social worker, is aimed at enabling the recognition and acceptance of loss, providing support through the period of sorrow and meaninglessness, and encouraging the bereaved to develop new relationships and a modified role. While the tasks of the bereaved derive from carrying out their 'grief-work', social workers should be aware of ways in which they may be helped to do this. The alternatives include individual social work help, group work, using community resources, and educating social networks. Throughout, there should be an attempt to modify personal and group attitudes towards death in order to develop public confidence. This will help to facilitate appropriate responses rather than an avoidance of the bereaved or rigid expectations which are derived from embarrassment and uncertainty.

8
Summary and Conclusions

Inside the narrow skull of the miner pinned beneath the fallen timber, there lives a world. Parents, friends, a home, the hot soup of evening, songs sung on feast days, loving kindness and anger, perhaps even a social consciousness and a great universal love, inhabit that skull ... Though we die for it, we shall bring up that miner from his shaft.

Antoine de Saint-Exupery, *Wind, Sand and Stars* (1939)

In Chapter 1, I commented that the purpose of this book was not only to explain how social workers might help the dying and bereaved, but to demonstrate why I think they have a particular contribution to make in this field of work. My view that social work has a vital role in relation to death and bereavement is based on three related lines of argument. First, I consider that any human experience must be appreciated within a framework which recognises the conscious, intentional and social nature of an individual's activities as he interacts with others. This approach demands that any researcher or social work practitioner attempts to understand the meaning of human actions and the process through which such meaning is created and validated in a social world. Clearly, the way in which I interpret the responses of dying patients, their relatives, and the bereaved, differs sharply from that which might be expected from a writer inclined towards psychoanalytic explanation. I would thus take issue with Pincus's emphasis on regression to child-like or primitive states as a response to loss, and her conclusion that the illustrations which she provides, 'are not esoteric fantasies of middle-class people who are familiar with psychological concepts but deep-rooted, age-old phenomena arising from unconscious processes, which can be found in the Bible, mythology and legends' (Pincus, 1976, p. 209). The reader should not conclude from my remarks that I believe all human behaviour to be conscious, intentional, and to have some meaning which may be recognised and expressed. However, what has been observed and recorded about the reactions of the dying and bereaved may be readily understood in terms of meaning and the process of social interaction.

Second, while there are problems in reaching a satisfactory definition of social work, I believe that it may be differentiated from other forms of professional intervention by an emphasis on social interaction and meaning. Such a focus requires that the social worker should have knowledge derived from empirical investigation, interpretative frameworks which enable the worker to make sense of data from this source, and accumulated evidence and experience concerning the effects of social work intervention. In the case of dying and bereavement, results of empirical investigations alert us to commonly occurring reactions, deviations from what might normally be expected, and the significance of various factors which influence the likelihood of successful resolution. An interpretative framework, based on an appreciation of social interaction and meaning, directs our attention to the social implications of loss, the social context in which death and bereavement occur, and the breakdown of taken-for-granted reality. A concentration on the effects (rather than effectiveness) of social work intervention, requires that we pay attention to the client's assessment, the social worker's presentation of self, the negotiation of conditions which govern the giving and acceptance of help, the development of a relationship, and the agreement of goals and work to be carried out. A psychoanalytic approach to dying and bereavement fails to attend to these points, because it neglects the social significance of loss and views individual responses as largely determined by progression or regression through a hierarchy of developmental stages. I would suggest that it is the business of social work to concentrate on those areas of human activity which are particularly social. This is not to suggest that instincts, drives or the internal functioning of the psyche have no relevance for understanding behaviour, but to point out that social work must concern itself with other matters if it is not to simply mirror the approaches of other related disciplines. Social work's unique contribution is not derived from a dependence on empirical investigation, theory, or experience and practice, but from the way in which these three areas are related to action, interaction, the social context in which these occur, and the work or practice issues of social intervention. If, as I have argued, social work is to do with knowledge, understanding and action in relation to the social context of clients' problems, and if dying and bereavement are viewed as social 'events', then clearly social workers have a contribution to make in this area of work.

Third, it could be argued that a sensitive social network of family and friends, is just as effective in helping the dying and bereaved as any social work service. This is undoubtedly true. The crucial point, however, is that while social workers have a professional responsibility to acquire relevant knowledge and to act in an appropriate way; family and friends do not. Friends and relatives can be forgiven for their embarrassment and uncertainty about how to approach the dying or bereaved, for the well-intentioned but unhelpful comments, and for the anxiety about getting out of their depth which leads them to discourage the expression of intense feelings. They may feel compassionate and altruistic, but lack the knowledge, confidence and self-awareness, which social workers should rightly be expected to acquire. Timms and Timms (1977, p. 47) have illustrated this point by suggesting that social work is 'altruism that is systematic, self-conscious and practised under social auspices'. It is this particular type of altruism (although Timms and Timms recognise the problems of this definition) which differentiates social work practice from help which is available through normal social networks. The statement of this distinction is relatively simple; the purpose of this book has been to show how it may be put into practice in the context of social work with the dying, their families, and the bereaved. Ballard (1979, p. 124) remarks that professional helping relationships may become more rewarding 'by the humaneness of what goes on when one person quite simply sits down with another and offers open comfort and understanding'. This sounds deceptively easy. However, in order to offer such comfort and understanding, the social worker needs to develop that degree of confidence, awareness of self and others, and the ability to 'sit down' with people who are in despair which enables an acceptance and tolerance of emotional pain. Doing something to make things better, or promising a happier time ahead, avoids the immediate feeling and expression of pain, anger, frustration, futility, and so on. Much of the social worker's professional responsibility in helping the dying and bereaved, hinges on an ability to recognise and eschew a tendency towards activity and optimism in a situation which requires facing pain and accepting despair.

I have attempted to distinguish between assumptions about certain things and what is known to be the case. In relation to this theme, I have carefully avoided any mention of the place of empathy in working with the dying and bereaved. In case the reader has noticed the absence of this commonly used term, I should explain my reticence about assuming its importance in social work practice. Corazzini suggests that empathy is a necessary skill for bereavement counsellors. The practice of empathy has two parts. First, the counsellor must 'experience the state of the bereaved person with the myriad feelings that accompany loss', and second, the counsellor should 'communicate the awareness of the state and its concomitant feelings to the grieving person' (Corazzini, 1980, p. 76). Paul (1967, p. 155) also draws attention to two aspects of empathy in the resolution of grief. He asserts that 'the empathizer is not only aware of the other's various experiences but finds himself sharing and reliving those experiences'. I consider it glib and of questionable validity to suggest that a social worker can *experience* the emotional state of someone who is dying or bereaved. What the worker can do, because she shares the same inter-subjective and symbolic world with others, is to grasp the meaning of their situation and the way in which they perceive this. Such an approach emphasises the importance of a concern to understand, rather than the fallacious assumption that a worker can 'live' the emotional experience of another. Even if the social worker has suffered a bereavement, or the counsellor is someone akin to a 'widow caregiver', their personal experience of loss does not necessarily enable them to feel exactly as another is feeling. They may be able to grasp the meaning and significance of loss more immediately and their offer of help may be more acceptable to those who are bereaved. The crucial nature of loss, however, lies in the essentially personal experience of those who are left. The challenge for social work lies in the ability to 'be with' the dying and bereaved through an expression of concern and understanding; the worker may feel for and with a client, but cannot live the other's experience. Neither is it necessarily helpful to assume that a social worker should try to empathise in the sense described above. For a worker to suggest that she can experience the feelings of someone who is bereaved serves only to minimise or deny the intensity of the other's response to loss and the nature of their essential aloneness. It should also be recognised that one of the worker's tasks is to represent and confirm that sense of stability, reliability and continuity, which the dying and bereaved have lost. This can only be achieved if the worker is perceived as being willing to accept and tolerate pain, while being firmly located in a world which is beyond the personal chaos engendered by actual and potential loss.

Having concluded that social workers do have a vital role in helping the dying and bereaved, it is now possible to summarise the knowledge and practice components of their contribution.

First, social workers require *knowledge* about:

1. Empirical investigations concerning the reactions of the dying and bereaved and the relative vulnerability of particular groups of clients.
2. The interpretation of data which provides a framework for 'making sense' of available information.
3. The context of intervention and questions of status, power,

decision-making responsibility, organisational requirements, and agency policy.
4. Presentation of self, personal and professional experience of and attitudes to loss, and the spiritual significance of dying and bereavement.

Second, social workers should consider their *focus of intervention*:

1. The individual; the dying and the bereaved.
2. The group; the dying and bereaved, the family, social networks, community resources.
3. Other professional workers; medical personnel in the hospital or community, DHSS, housing, social workers.
4. The public; indirect intervention through changing attitudes and increasing awareness of death and bereavement.
5. The organisation; influencing policies, the allocation of resources.

Third, social workers should act in such a way as to *be perceived as being*:

1. Trustworthy; will not avoid distress or minimise the client's pain.
2. Reliable; will not withdraw, be judgemental, be overwhelmed; will come back.
3. Confident; will not be alarmed, embarrassed, or uncertain.
4. Concerned; will be available, attentive, responsive to cues.
5. Understanding; will attempt to grasp the meaning of this situation and experience for the individual(s) concerned.

Fourth, social workers *should be able to*:

1. Communicate; verbally and non-verbally with clients and professional colleagues.
2. Analyse; break down a problem into identifiable and manageable parts.
3. Enable; the release of feelings without fear of loss of control.
4. Accept; anger, pain, despair; without avoidance, denial, being judgemental.
5. Explain; the client's perceptions, needs and feelings to others.
6. Clarify; processes of interaction between clients and others, within groups.

7. Encourage; acceptance of loss, making new relationships, development of control and self-esteem.
8. Let go; set goals, accept alternative sources of help, allow independence, terminate contact.

All this requires that the social worker pays close attention to questions of meaning, social interaction and the way in which reality is perceived, constructed and confirmed by self and others. The list of things which a social worker should know and be able to do may seem formidable. It is, however, similar to any summary of knowledge and practice in other areas of social work intervention. Working with the dying and bereaved does not require any unique or novel techniques. It does demand that the worker is prepared to face some fundamental questions about death and loss and to seek out appropriate knowledge. Having said this, I would conclude that techniques of social work intervention are as applicable to helping the dying and bereaved as any other client group. Timms and Timms (1977, p. 87) have clearly recognised the importance of this point when they suggest that social workers should be able to 'conduct interviews with individuals or groups who often face and experience loss and change'. I have argued that the experience of loss involves both social worker and client in grappling with the question of meaning and a disruption of taken-for-granted reality and identity. Viewed in this way, social workers are continually dealing with actual or potential loss. They may be removing a child from natural parents, helping an elderly client to make a decision about moving into residential care, or working with a group of people who must be rehoused away from a familiar and close-knit community. With the increasing significance of adoption in planning for children who need permanent family placements, there have been efforts to develop ways of helping children to understand and cope with the loss of familiar settings and their natural family. It is recognised that older children will need to review past experiences, to develop the kind of historical and emotional perspective which was referred to earlier, and to express their anger and sadness, if they are to be adequately prepared for joining adoptive families. Such preparation is essential to enable these children to develop new relationships, to establish a sense of trust and self-esteem, and to make an emotional investment in their new families.

Many of the experiences and responses which have been discussed during the course of this book will be apparent in situations involving loss. Appropriate social work techniques will be similar in many respects, whether the client is a dying patient, a bereaved relative, an older child who is moving into an adoptive home, a woman whose husband wants a divorce, and so on. While I have concentrated on social work with adults, the guiding principles concerning presentation of self and the application of appropriate techniques are equally relevant to working with children who may be dying or bereaved. Ballard (1979, p. 124) has suggested that parents of handicapped children 'will be able to forgive the professional blunders of doctors, nurses, social workers, and health visitors' if they are approached with 'respect, consideration, warmth and care'. Respect and care involve the social worker in ensuring that she has relevant knowledge and a grasp of appropriate social work practice.

A Guide to Further Reading

Chapter 1

Miller and Acri (1977) have written an extensive bibliography which includes references to a wide range of contributions on death, dying and bereavement. Prichard *et al.* (1977) and Schoenberg *et al.* (1974) contain some useful articles on the importance of social work help for the dying and bereaved. For a helpful introductory book on some of the professional issues facing social workers, see Timms and Timms (1977), and for a discussion of the relevance of systems theory to social work practice, see Goldstein (1973), Pincus and Minahan (1973), Specht and Vickery (1977), Hearn (1979). The importance and difficulties of inter-professional co-operation are highlighted by Toff (1979) and Nursing Times Service (1973). Readers who may be interested in exploring the problems faced by families and medical personnel who are caring for handicapped and terminally ill children are referred to Burton (1974 and 1975), Elfer (1979), Davis (1963), Kaplan *et al.* (1973), Fields (1977).

Chapter 2

Detailed discussions of problems relating to theory and research in the social sciences may be found in Rex (1961), Hamilton (1974), Curtis and Petras (1970), Filstead (1970), Phillips (1973). Research concerning communication between doctors, patients and their families has been reported by Mechanic (1961), Korsch *et al.* (1968), Maguire and Rutter (1976), Ley (1976), Cartwright (1964), Boyle (1975). Communication between medical personnel and those who are terminally ill has also been discussed by Oken (1961), Hinton (1967), McIntosh (1977), Parkes (1977). The reactions of children to hospitalisation and serious illness has been explored by Natterson and Knudson (1960), Fields (1977), Elfer (1979). Kalish (1966), Weisman and Hackett (1961), Hinton (1967), and Kübler-Ross (1970), have all discussed the reactions of family and friends to someone who is terminally ill and the way in which this can increase the patient's sense of isolation and distress.

Chapter 3

Parkes (1972) provides a good overview of the literature and research studies concerning reactions to bereavement, and Prichard *et al.* (1977) contains several useful articles on this subject. For a discussion of how Japanese culture and religion may influence reactions to bereavement, see Yamamoto *et al.* (1969). Parkes (1964), Wiener *et al.* (1975), Maddison and Viola (1968), have all explored the relationship between bereavement and increased consultation with general practitioners for physical and psychological problems, while the relationship between loss and the onset of psychiatric disorders has been discussed by Brown (1974), Brown *et al.* (1975), Paykel (1974), Stein and Susser (1969).

Chapter 4

Readers who would like to consider Freud's ideas in depth, are referred to his works of 1912–13, 1915, 1917 and 1926. Klein's contribution to this subject is discussed in her book of 1963, and in Klein and Riviere (1967). Bowlby's criticisms of Freud, and his own discussion about instinct-based explanations of attachment behaviour and reactions to loss, may be found in his work of 1961, 1969, 1973 and 1980. If the reader is interested in the approach of symbolic interactionism and phenomenology, helpful discussion, including criticisms, can be found in Schutz (1972), Giddens (1976), Gorman (1975), Meltzer *et al.* (1975), Hamilton (1974). Blumer (1969) and Mead (1934) explore the 'I' and 'Me' elements of personality in relation to sociological investigation and explanation.

For further discussion of the relationship between mental illness and difficulties in the development of identity through social interaction, see Becker (1975) and Rose (1975). Some writers have concentrated on the loss of meaningful activity and roles during middle age (Parent, 1977), as the result of amputation (Dembo *et al.*, 1952, and Fisher, 1960), and through community disruption (Fried, 1962). The implications of crisis theory have been given detailed attention by Caplan (1964), Parad (1965), Rapoport (1970), Golan (1978 and 1979). Lerner (1975) provides a good historical description of the ways in which the social and institutional management of mourning have changed and become less clearly defined.

Chapter 5

For a discussion of the patient role and the ways in which patients and medical practitioners negotiate appropriate behaviour and expectations, the reader is referred to Bloom and Wilson (1972), Roth (1963), Freidson (1970), Tuckett (1976). Attention has been given to organisational requirements of patient care and the importance of technical competence in medical personnel by Rosengren and De Vault (1963) and Sudnow (1967).

Helpful books about social work interviews and techniques required for successful interviewing have been written by Cross (1974) and Kadushin (1972). There are also some useful sections on this topic in Haines (1975), and Timms and Timms (1977). Kübler-Ross (1970) and McIntosh (1977) contain some excellent discussions on the terminally ill patient's need to retain hope and the balance between the maintenance of hope and a desire to seek information about diagnosis and prognosis. Parfit (1971) provides a useful review of group work with clients who have specific problems.

Chapter 6

Sudnow (1967) provides a very good analysis of the ways in which doctors and relatives act when information about terminal illness is being imparted. For a helpful discussion of problems associated with telling children about their own or other's terminal conditions the reader is referred to Kaplan (1973), and useful papers in Burton (1974) and Schoenberg *et al.* (1975).

See Paul (1967 and 1973), and Paul and Grosser (1965) for detailed discussion of family therapy where a member is dying or has died.

Chapter 7

Craig (1977) has written an interesting and thought-provoking article on parents' search for meaning following the death of a child, particularly with reference to spiritual questions. Schiff's (1977) account of her personal experience of the death of her son is direct, compassionate and of immense help to those who wish to understand and work with the bereaved. For a useful source of material and further references concerning bereavement, the reader can choose among a number of papers in Schoenberg (1980) and Schoenberg *et al.* (1975).

Chapter 8

The situation in which older children are moving into adoptive families and facing the loss of natural parents, familiar people and environments and have already experienced the loss of self-esteem, trust and confidence, is enlightening when considered in relation to losses involved in death and bereavement. Those readers who would like to explore this topic further will find useful discussions in Unger *et al.* (1977), Jewett (1978), Lightbown (1979).

References

Ablon, J. (1971) 'Bereavement in a Samoan community', *British Journal of Medical Psychology*, 44, 329.

Aitken-Swan, J. (1959) 'Nursing the late cancer patient at home', *The Practitioner*, 183, July, pp. 64–9.

Aldrich, C. K. (1963) 'The dying patient's grief', *Journal of the American Medical Association*, 184 (5), pp. 329–31.

Balint, M. (1964) *The Doctor, His Patient and the Illness*, London, Pitman Medical.

Ballard, R. (1979) 'Face to face with the unthinkable', in G. Lonsdale *et al.*, *Children, Grief and Social Work*, Oxford, Blackwell, pp. 115–25.

Battin, D. *et al.* (1977) 'Clinical observations on bereaved individuals', in E. R. Prichard *et al.* (eds), *Social Work with the Dying Patient and the Family*, New York, Columbia University Press, pp. 80–95.

Becker, E. (1975) 'Socialisation, command of performance and mental illness', in C. Cox and A. Mead (eds), *A Sociology of Medical Practice*, New York, Collier-Macmillan, pp. 62–73.

Becker, H. S. (ed.) (1964) *The Other Side: Perspectives on Deviance*, New York, Collier-Macmillan.

Benoliel, J. Q. (1974) 'Anticipatory grief in physicians and nurses', in B. Schoenberg *et al.* (eds), *Anticipatory Grief*, New York, Columbia University Press, pp. 218–28.

Berger, P. and Kellner, H. (1970) 'Marriage and the construction of reality', in H. P. Dreitzel (ed.), *Recent Sociology No. 2*, New York, Collier-Macmillan.

Berger, P. and Luckmann, T. (1967) *The Social Construction of Reality*, Harmondsworth, Penguin.

Bloom, S. W. and Wilson, R. N. (1972) 'Patient–practitioner relationships', in H. E. Freeman *et al.* (eds), *Handbook of Medical Sociology*, Englewood Cliffs, N. J., Prentice-Hall.

Blumer, H. (1969) *Symbolic Interactionism: Perspective and Method*, Englewood Cliffs, N. J., Prentice-Hall.

Bornstein, P. E. *et al.*, (1973) 'The depression of widowhood after 13 months', *British Journal of Psychology*, 122, p. 561.

Bowlby, J. (1961) 'Childhood mourning and its implications for psychiatry', *American Journal of Psychiatry*, 118, p. 481.

Bowlby, J. (1961) 'Processes of mourning', *International Journal of Psychoanalysis*, 13, p. 22.

Bowlby, J. (1969) *Attachment and Loss: Vol. 1 Attachment*, London, Hogarth Press and the Institute of Psychoanalysis.

Bowlby, J. (1973) *Attachment and Loss: Vol. 2 Separation*, London, Hogarth Press and the Institute of Psychoanalysis.

Bowlby, J. (1980) *Attachment and Loss: Vol. 3 Loss*, London, Hogarth Press.

Boyle, C. M. (1975) 'Differences between patients' and doctors' interpretations of some common medical terms', in C. Cox and A. Mead (eds), *A Sociology of Medical Practice*, New York, Collier-Macmillan, pp. 299—308.

British Association of Social Workers (1977 *The Social Work Task*, Birmingham, BASW.

British Medical Journal (1973) 'Contemporary Themes: Care of the Dying', *British Medical Journal*, 6 January, pp. 29—40.

Brown, G. W. (1974) 'Meaning, measurement and stress of life-events', in B. S. Dohrenwend and B. P. Dohrenwend (eds), *Stressful Life Events: Their Nature and Effects*, New York, Wiley.

Brown, G. W. *et al.* (1975) 'Social class and psychiatric disturbance among women in an urban population', *Sociology*, 9, p. 225.

Brown, G. W. *et al.* (1979) 'Depression and loss', in P. Williams and A. Clare (eds), *Psycho-social Disorders in General Practice*, New York, Academic Press, p. 85.

Burnage, A. (1976) 'The social problems of the infertile', unpublished MSc, Nottingham University.

Burton, L. (1974) (ed.), *Care of the Child Facing Death*, London, Routledge & Kegan Paul.

Burton, L. (1975) *The Family Life of Sick Children*, London, Routledge & Kegan Paul.

Busfield, J. and Padden, M. (1977) *Thinking about Children*, Cambridge University Press.

Caplan, G. (1964) *Principles of Preventive Psychiatry*, New York, Basic Books.

Cartwright, A. (1964) *Human Relations and Hospital Care*, London, Routledge & Kegan Paul.

Cartwright A. *et al.* (1973) *Life before Death*, London, Routledge & Kegan Paul.

Clayton, P. *et al.* (1968) 'A study of normal bereavement', *American Journal of Psychiatry*, 125(2), p. 168.

Cohen, P. *et al.* (1977) 'Family adaptation to terminal illness and death of a parent', *Social Casework*, April, pp. 223–8.

Cooper, J. (1980) 'Parental reaction to stillbirth', *British Journal of Social Work*, 10, p. 55.

Corazzini, J. G. (1980) 'The theory and practice of loss therapy', in B. Schoenberg (ed.), *Bereavement Counselling*, London, Greenwood Press, pp. 71–85.

Craig, Y. (1977) 'The bereavement of parents and their search for meaning', *British Journal of Social Work*, 7(1), pp. 41–54.

Cross, C. P. (ed.) (1974) *Interviewing and Communication in Social Work*, London, Routledge & Kegan Paul.

Curtis, J. E. and Petras, J. W. (eds) (1970) *The Sociology of Knowledge: a Reader*, New York, Praeger.

Das, S. (1971) 'Grief and the imminent threat of non-being', *British Journal of Psychiatry*, 118, pp. 467–8.

Davis, F. (1963) *Passage through Crisis*, Indianapolis, Bobbs-Merrill.

Dembo, T. *et al.* (1952) 'Acceptance of loss: amputation', in J. F. Garrett (ed.), *Psychological Aspects of Physical Disabilities*, Washington, U. S. Govt Printing Office.

Elfer, P. (1979) 'Social work with children with leukaemia and their families', in G. Lonsdale *et al.*, *Children, Grief and Social Work*, Oxford, Blackwell.

Engel, G. L. (1961) 'Is grief a disease?', *Psychosomatic Medicine*, 13(1), p. 19.

Evans, R. (1976) 'Some implications of an integrated model of social work for theory and practice', *British Journal of Social Work*, 6(2), pp. 177–200.

Fields, G. (1977) 'The dying child and his family', in E. R. Prichard *et al.* (eds) *Social Work with the Dying Patient and the Family*, New York, Columbia University Press, pp. 124–30.

Filstead, W. J. (ed.) (1970) *Qualitative Methodology*, Chicago, Markham.

Fisher, S. H. (1960) 'Psychiatric considerations of hand disability', *Archives of Physical Medicine and Rehabilitation*, 41, p. 62.

Fitzjohn, J. (1974) 'An interactionist view of the social work interview', *British Journal of Social Work*, 4(4), p. 425.

Forder, A. (1976) 'Social work and system theory', *British Journal of Social Work*, 6(1), pp. 23–42.

Freidson, E. (1970) *Professions of Medicine*, New York, Dodd, Mead & Co.

Freud, S. (1912–13) 'Totem and taboo', *Standard Edition*, vol. 13, London, Hogarth Press.

Freud, S. (1915) 'Instincts and their vicissitudes', *Standard Edition*, vol. 14, London, Hogarth Press.

Freud, S. (1917) 'Mourning and melancholia', *Standard Edition*, vol. 14, London, Hogarth Press.

Freud, S. (1926) 'Inhibitions, symptoms and anxiety', *Standard Edition*, vol. 20, London, Hogarth Press.

Freund, J. (1977) 'When should the clergyman be called?', in E. R. Prichard *et al.* (eds), *Social Work with the Dying Patient and the Family*, pp. 208–16.

Fried, M. (1962) 'Grieving for a lost home', in L. J. Duhl (ed.), *The Environment of the Metropolis*, New York, Basic Books.

Garfinkel, H. (1967) 'Studies of the routine grounds of everyday activities', *Studies in Ethnomethodology*, Englewood Cliffs, N.J. Prentice-Hall.

Gerber, I. (1974) 'Anticipatory bereavement', in B. Schoenberg *et al.* (eds), *Anticipatory Grief*, pp. 26–30.

Gerber, I. *et al.* (1975) 'Brief therapy to the aged bereaved', in B. Schoenberg *et al.* (eds), *Bereavement: Its Psycho-social Aspects*, New York, Columbia University Press pp. 310–34.

Giddens, A. (1976) *New Rules of Sociological Method*, London, Hutchinson.

Ginsberg, L. H. (1977) 'The social worker's role', in E. R. Prichard *et al.* (eds), *Social Work with the Dying Patient and the Family*, pp. 3–11.

Goffman, E. (1959) *Presentation of Self in Everyday Life*, New York, Doubleday.

Goffman, E. (1963) *Stigma*, Englewood Cliffs, N.J., Prentice-Hall.

Golan, N. (1978) *Treatment in Crisis Situations*, New York, Free Press.

Golan, N. (1979) 'Crisis theory in social work treatment', in F. J. Turner (ed.) *Social Work Treatment*, New York, Collier-Macmillan p. 499.

Goldberg, S. B. (1973) 'Family task and reactions in the crisis of death', *Social Casework*, 54, July, pp. 398–405.

Goldstein, H. (1973) Social Work Practice: a Unitary Approach, University of South Carolina Press.

Goodyear, C. P. (1977) 'Group therapy with advanced cancer patients' in E. R. Prichard *et al.*, *Social Work with the Dying Patient and the Family*, pp. 242–51.

Gorer, G. (1965) *Death, Grief and Mourning*, London, Cresset Press.

Gorman, R. H. (1975) 'Alfred Schutz—an exposition and critique', *British Journal of Sociology*, 26, p. 1.

Haines, J. (1975) *Skills and Methods in Social Work*, London, Constable.

Hamilton, P. (1974) *Knowledge and Social Structures*, London, Routledge & Kegan Paul.

Houghton P. and Houghton D. (1977) *Unfocused Grief*, The Birmingham Settlement.

Hearn, G. (1979) 'General systems theory and social work', in F. J. Turner (ed.), *Social Work Treatment*, pp. 333–59.

Hinton, J. M. (1963) 'The physical and mental distress of the dying', *Quarterly Journal of Medicine*, 32, pp. 1–21.

Hinton, J. M. (1967) *Dying*, Hamondsworth, Penguin.

Hughes, H. L. G. (1960) *Peace at the Last: a Survey of Terminal Care in the UK*, London, Calouste Gulbenkian Foundation.

Jeffreys, M. (1975) 'The doctor's dilemma a sociological viewpoint', in C. Cox and A. Mead (eds), *A Sociology of Medical Practice*, pp. 145–55.

Jewett, C. L. (1978) *Adopting the Older Child*, Harvard, Common Press.

Jones, W. H. (1977) 'Death-related grief counselling: the school counsellor's responsibility', *School Counsellor*, 24, pp. 315–20.

Jordan, B. (1978) 'A comment on theory and practice in social work', *British Journal of Social Work*, 8(1), pp. 23–5.

Kadushin, A. (1972) *The Social Work Interview*, New York, Columbia University Press.

Kalish, R. A. (1966) 'Social distance and the dying', *Community Mental Health Journal*, 2, p. 152.

Kaplan, D. M. *et al.* (1973) 'Family mediation of stress', *Social Work*, July, pp. 60–9.

Kincey, V. (1974) 'The evaluation of a bereavement counselling service', MSc. thesis, University of Manchester.

Klein, M. (1963) *Our Adult World and its Roots in Infancy and Other Essays*, London, Heinemann.

Klein, M. and Riviere, J. (1967) *Love, Hate and Reparation*, London, Hogarth Press and the Institute of Psychoanalysis.

Knott, B. H. (1974) 'Social work as symbolic interaction', *British Journal of Social Work*, 4(1), p. 5.

Korsch, B. H. *et al.* (1968) 'Gaps in doctor–patient communication', *Paediatrics*, 42(5), pp. 855–69.

Kübler-Ross, E. (1970) *On Death and Dying*, London, Tavistock.

Lack, S. and Lamerton, R. (1974) *The Hour of Our Death*, London, Chapman.

Leared, J. (1978) 'Bereavement and mourning', *Social Work Today*, 9(45), July, pp. 16–17.

Leighton, N. (1973) 'The act of understanding', *British Journal of Social Work*, 3(4), p. 509.

Leonard, P. (1975) 'Explanation and education in social work', *British Journal of Social Work*, 5(3), pp. 325–33.

Lerner, J. C. (1975) 'Changes in attitudes towards death', in B. Schoenberg *et al.* (eds), *Bereavement*, pp. 91–119.

Ley, P. (1976) 'Towards better doctor—patient communication', in E. A. Bennett (ed.) *Communication between Doctors and Patients*, Oxford University Press, pp. 77—97.

Lightbown, C. (1979) 'Life story books', *Adoption and Fostering*, 97, pp. 9—15.

Lindemann, E. (1944) 'Symptomatology and management of acute grief', *American Journal of Psychiatry*, 101, p. 141.

Lonsdale, G. *et al.* (1979) *Children, Grief and Social Work*, Oxford, Blackwell.

McIntosh, J. (1979) *Communication and Awareness on a Cancer Ward*, London, Croom Helm.

Maddison, D. (1968) 'The relevance of conjugal bereavement for preventive psychiatry', *British Journal of Medical Psychology*, 41, p. 223.

Maddison, D. and Raphael, B. (1975) 'Conjugal bereavement and the social network', in B. Schoenberg *et al.* (eds), *Bereavement*, pp. 26—41.

Maddison, D. and Viola, A. (1968) 'The health of widows in the year following bereavement', *Journal of Psychosomatic Research*, 12, p. 297.

Maddison, D. and Walker, W. L. (1967) 'Factors affecting the outcome of conjugal bereavement', *British Journal of Psychology*, 113, p. 1057.

Maguire, G. P. and Rutter, D. (1976) 'Training medical students to communicate', in E. A. Bennett (ed.), *Communication between Doctors and Patients*, pp. 47—74.

Marris, P. (1958) *Widows and Their Families*, London, Routledge & Kegan Paul.

Marris, P. (1974) *Loss and Change*, London, Routledge & Kegan Paul.

Mayer, J. and Timms, N. (1970) *The Client Speaks*, London, Routledge & Kegan Paul.

Mead, G. H. (1934) *Mind, Self and Society*, University of Chicago Press.

Mechanic, D. (1961) 'Role expectations and communications in the therapist—patient relationship', *Journal of Health and Social Behaviour*, p. 194.

Meltzer, B. N. *et al.* (1975) *Symbolic Interactionism*, London, Routledge & Kegan Paul.

Middlestadt, E. (1978) 'Using adoptive parents', *Adoption and Fostering*, 93, pp. 18—22.

Miller, A. J. and Acri, M. J. (1977) *Death: a Bibliographical Guide*, Metuchen, N.J., Scarecrow Press.

Natanson, M. (1970) *The Journeying Self*, Reading, Mass., Addison-Wesley.

Natterson, J. M. and Knudson, A. G. (1960) 'Observations concerning fear of death in fatally ill children and their mothers', *Psychosomatic Medicine*, 22, p. 456.

Neilson, J. (1979) 'Placing older children in adoptive homes', *No Child is Unadoptable*, Beverley Hills, California, Sage.

Nursing Times Service (1973) *Terminal Care*, London, Macmillan Journals.

Oken, D. (1961) 'What to tell cancer patients', *Journal of the American Medical Association*, 175, p. 1120.

Orcutt, B. A. (1977) 'Stress in family interaction when a member is dying', in E. R. Prichard *et al.* (eds), *Social Work with the Dying Patient and the Family*, pp. 23–8.

Palmer, T. (1973) 'Matching worker and client in connections', *Social Work*, 18, pp. 95–103.

Parent, M. K. (1977) 'The losses of middle age and related developmental tasks', in E. R. Prichard *et al.* (eds), *Social Work with the Dying Patient and the Family*, pp. 146–54.

Parfit, J. (1971) *Group Work with Parents in Special Circumstances*, London, National Children's Bureau.

Parkes, C. M. (1964) 'The effects of bereavement on physical and mental health', *British Medical Journal*, 2, p. 274.

Parkes, C. M. (1965a) 'Bereavement and mental illness, part I', *British Journal of Medical Psychology*, 38(1), p. 1.

Parkes, C. M. (1965b) 'Bereavement and mental illness, part II', *British Journal of Medical Psychology*, 38, p. 13.

Parkes, C. M. (1972) *Bereavement: Studies of Grief in Adult Life*, London, Tavistock.

Parkes, C. M. (1975) 'Unexpected and untimely bereavement, a study of young Boston widows and widowers', in B. Schoenberg *et al.* (eds), *Bereavement*, pp. 119–38.

Parkes, C. M. (1977) 'Evaluation of family care in terminal illness', in E. R. Prichard *et al.* (eds), *Social Work with the Dying Patient and the Family*, pp. 49–79.

Parad, H. J. (ed.) (1965) *Crisis Intervention: Selected Readings*, New York, Family Service Association of America.

Paul, N. L. (1967) 'The use of empathy in the resolution of grief', *Perspectives in Biology and Medicine*, 2, pp. 153–68.

Paul, N. L. (1973) 'The need to mourn', in E. J. Anthony and C. Koupernick (eds), *The Child in His Family*, vol. 2, New York, Wiley, pp. 219–24.

Paul, N. P. and Grosser, G. H. (1965) 'Operational mourning and its role in cojoint family therapy', *Community Mental Health Journal*, 1, pp. 339–45.

Paykel, E. S. (1974) 'Recent life-events and clinical depression', in

E. K. E. Gunderson and R. H. Rahe (eds), *Life, Stress and Illness*, Springfield, Ill., Charles C. Thomas.

Phillips, D. L. (1973) *Abandoning Method*, San Francisco, Jossey Bass.

Pincus, A. and Minahan, A. (1973) *Social Work Practice: Model and Method*, Illinois, Peacock Press.

Pincus, A. and Minahan, A. (1977) 'A model for social work practice', in H. Specht and A. Vickery (eds), *Integrating Social Work Methods*, London, Allen & Unwin, pp. 73–108.

Pincus, L. (1976) *Death and the Family*, London, Faber & Faber.

Plummer, K. (1975) *Sexual Stigma*, London, Routledge & Kegan Paul.

Polak, P. R. *et al.* (1973) 'Crisis intervention in acute bereavement', Colorado, draft paper from Fort Logan Community Mental Health Centre.

Pollack, G. H. (1961) 'Mourning and adaptation', *International Journal of Psychoanalysis*, 42, p. 341.

Prichard, E. R. *et al.* (eds) (1977) *Social Work with the Dying Patient and the Family*, New York, Columbia University Press.

Raphael, B. (1977) 'Preventive intervention with the recently bereaved', *Archives of General Psychology*, 34, pp. 1450–4.

Raphael, B. (1980) 'A psychiatric model for bereavement counselling', in B. M. Schoenberg (ed.), *Bereavement Counselling*, pp. 147–72.

Rapoport, L. (1970) 'Crisis intervention as a mode of treatment', in R. W. Roberts and R. H. Nee (eds), *Theories of Social Casework*, University of Chicago Press, pp. 267–311.

Rex, J. (1961) *Key Problems of Sociological Theory*, London, Routledge & Kegan Paul.

Robinson, D. (1973) *Patients, Practitioners and Medical Care*, London, Heinemann.

Roche, E. (1979) *The Widow, Her Children and Their Worlds*, Essex, Dr Barnardo's.

Rose, A. M. (1975 'A social-psychological theory of neurosis', in C. Cox and A. Mead (eds), *A Sociology of Medical Practice*, pp. 74–83.

Rosengren, W. and De Vault, S. (1963) 'The sociology of time and space in an obstetrical hospital', in E. Freidson (ed.), *The Hospital in Modern Society*, New York, Free Press.

Roth, J. A. (1963) *Timetables*, Indianapolis, Bobbs-Merrill.

Rutter, M. (1972) *Maternal Deprivation Reassessed*, Harmondsworth, Penguin.

Rutter, M (1976) 'Parent–child separation: psychological effects on the children', in A. M. Clarke and A. D. B. Clarke (eds), *Early Experience: Myth and Evidence*, London, Open Books.

Salzberger-Wittenberg, I. (1970) *Psychoanalytic Insight and Relationships: a Kleinian Approach*, London, Routledge & Kegan Paul.

Saunders, C. (1959) *Care of the Dying*, London, Macmillan.

Saunders, C. (1973) 'A Death in the Family: a Professional View', *British Medical Journal*, 6 January.

Saunders, C. (1974) 'Caring for the dying', in S. Lack and R. Lamerton (eds), *The Hour of Our Death*, London, Chapman, pp. 18—27.

Schiff, H. S. (1977) *The Bereaved Parent*, New York, Crown.

Schoenberg, B. *et al.* (1974) *Anticipatory Grief*, New York, Columbia University Press.

Schoenberg, B. (ed.) (1980) *Bereavement Counselling*, London, Greenwood Press.

Schoenberg, B. *et al.* (1975) *Bereavement: its Psycho-Social Aspects*, New York, Columbia University Press.

Schowalter, J. E. (1975) 'Parent death and child bereavement', in B. M. Schoenberg *et al.* (eds), *Bereavement*, pp. 172—9.

Schutz, A. (1972) *The Phenomenology of the Social World*, London, Heinemann.

Schutz, A. and Luckmann, T. (1976) *The Structure of the Life-World*, London, Heinemann.

Schwab, J. J. *et al.* (1975) 'Studies in grief: a preliminary report', in Schoenberg *et al.* (eds), *Bereavement*, pp. 78—90.

Sheldon, B. (1978) 'Theory and practice in social work: a re-examination of a tenuous relationship', *British Journal of Social Work*, 8(1), pp. 1—22.

Silverman, P. R. (1970) 'The widow as caregiver', *Mental Hygiene*, 54(4), October, pp. 540—7.

Smith, C. R. (1973) 'Medical social workers: essential experts or misplaced intruders?', *British Medical Journal*, 25 August, p. 443.

Smith, C. R. (1980) 'Adoption policy and practice', unpublished PhD thesis, Leeds University.

Specht, H. and Vickery, A. (eds) (1977) *Integrating Social Work Methods*, London, Allen & Unwin.

Stacey, M. *et al.* (1970) *Hospitals, Children and Their Families*, London, Routledge & Kegan Paul.

Steele, D. W. (1977) 'The counsellor's response to death', *Personnel and Guidance Journal*, 56, pp. 164—7.

Stein, Z. and Susser, M. W. (1969) 'Widowhood and mental illness', *British Journal of Preventive and Social Medicine*, p. 23.

Stockwell, F. (1972) *The Unpopular Patient*, London, Royal College of Nursing.

Strauss, A. L. and Glaser, B. G. (1975) 'Patterns of dying', in C. Cox and A. Mead (eds), *A Sociology of Medical Practice*, pp. 247—68.

Sudnow, D. (1967) *Passing On*, Englewood Cliffs, N.J., Prentice-Hall.

Szasz, T. (1972) *The Myth of Mental Illness*, London, Paladin.

Tallmer, M. (1975) 'Sexual and age factors in childhood bereavements', in B. M. Schoenberg *et al.* (eds), *Bereavement*, pp. 164—71.

Tessler, R. C. (1975) 'Clients' reactions to initial interviews', *Journal of Counselling Psychology*, 22(3), pp. 187—91.

Timms, N. and Timms, R. (1977) *Perspectives in Social Work*, London, Routledge & Kegan Paul.

Toff, J. (1979) 'According dignity to the dying', *Social Work Today*, 11(1).

Tuckett, D. (1976) *Medical Sociology*, London, Tavistock.

Unger, C. *et al.* (1977) *Chaos, Madness and Unpredictability*, Michigan, Spaulding.

Volkan, V. D. (1970) 'Typical findings in pathological grief', *Psychology Quarterly*, 44, p. 231.

Volkan, V. D. (1971) 'A study of a patient's re-grief work through dreams, psychological tests and psychoanalysis', *Psychology Quarterly*, 45, p. 222.

Volkan, V. D. (1975) 'Re-grief therapy', in B. Schoenberg *et al.* (eds), *Bereavement*, pp. 334—50.

Volkan, V. D. and Showalter, C. R. (1968) 'Known object loss, disturbance in reality testing, and re-grief work as a method of brief psychotherapy', *Psychology Quarterly*, 42, p. 358.

Vollman R. R. *et al.* (1971) 'The reactions of family systems to sudden and unexpected death', *Omega*, 67—106.

Weisman, A. D. and Hackett, T. P. (1961) 'Predilection to death', *Psychosomatic Medicine*, 23, p. 232.

Wiener, A. *et al.* (1975) 'The process and phenomenology of bereavement', in B. M. Schoenberg *et al.* (eds), *Bereavement*, pp. 53—65.

Williams, W. V. *et al.* (1972) 'Crisis intervention in acute grief', *Omega*, 3, pp. 67—70.

Yamamoto, J. *et al.* (1969) 'Mourning in Japan', *American Journal of Psychiatry*, 125(12), p. 1660.

Index

Ablon, J.   49
adoption and loss   92, 131, 132
Aitken-Swan, J.   16
Aldrich, C. K.   82
altruism   127

Balint, M.   19
Ballard, R.   132
Battin, D. *et al.*   27
Benoliel, J. Q.   8
bereavement
  adolescent   34
  anticipation of   30
  childhood   33
  health following   28
  preparation for   28, 29
  reactions to   25–7, 30–3
Berger, P. and Kellner, H.   47
Berger, P. and Luckmann, T.
  45
Bornstein, P. E. *et al.*   28
Brown, G. W. *et al.*   33
Burnage, A.   19–20
Busfield, J. and Padden, M.   7

Cartwright, A. *et al.*   14, 15, 19,
  21, 30
Clayton, P. *et al.*   27, 28
client perceptions   57, 58
Cohen, P. *et al.*   22, 36
communication
  of diagnosis   17, 18, 77

research studies   17, 61
social class   17
with children   100
with relatives   18, 21, 22, 98,
  99
community resources   123, 124
Cooper, J.   50
Corazzini, J. G.   116, 128
crisis   51, 52
Cross, C. P.   69

Das, S.   76
denial   20, 75, 76
dying
  acceptance   20, 22, 80
  anger   20, 78, 79
  bargaining   20
  denial   20
  depression   20, 79, 80
  loss   82, 86
  past experiences   82, 83
empathy   128, 129
Engel, G. L.   25

family
  communication   36, 37,
    102, 103
  mother's death   22, 23, 37
  roles   36, 37, 60
Fitzjohn, J.   55
Forder, A.   6

Freud, S. 39
Freund, J. 84

Garfinkel, H. 59
general practitioners (GPs) 15
Gerber, I. 30
Gerber, I. *et al.* 105
Ginsberg, L. H. 8
Goffman, E. 87
Goodyear, C. P. 86
Gorer, G. 25, 49
Goldberg, S. B. 36
groups 85–7

Hinton, J. 14, 17, 20, 21
home care 14–16, 96, 97
hope 75
Houghton, P. and Houghton, D. 55
Hughes, H. L. G. 14

identification 42
instincts 44, 45, 127
interpretation 6, 7, 126–32
interviewing 69–74
involuntary childlessness 55

Jeffreys, M. 19
Jones, W. H. 115
Jordan, B. 5

Kadushin, A. 88
Kaplan, D. M. *et al.* 22
Kincey, V. 105
Klein, M. 41
Knott, B. H. 55
Kübler-Ross, E. 8, 18, 20, 22, 84

language 45
Leared, J. 59
Leighton, N. 55
Leonard, P. 11
Lindemann, E. 25, 33, 40
Lonsdale, G. 91

McIntosh, J. 18, 61
Maddison, D. 35

Maddison, D. and Raphael, B. 35
marriage 47
Marris, P. 25, 50, 54
Mayer, J. and Timms, N. 6
mourning
    cultural factors 49
    historical factors 49
    in Japan 49
    in the USA 49

Natanson, M. 48
Neilson, J. 92

objective reality 45
Orcutt, B. A. 22

Palmer, T. 58
paranoid anxiety 41
Parkes, C. M. 16, 25, 26, 28, 29, 31, 32, 106
physical pain 16, 21
Pincus, A. and Minahan, A. 5, 8
Pincus, L. 41, 126, 127
Plummer, K. 48
Polak, P. R. *et al.* 105
Pollack, G. H. 40
presentation of self 57, 58, 88, 93, 115
prevention 105, 106
professions
    affective functions 63, 67, 68
    relationships 19, 23, 60, 61
    relative status 61–3, 67
    technical competence 18, 19, 60, 62, 63
projection 42
psychiatric illness 30–3
psychoanalytic theory 39, 42, 43, 126, 127

Raphael, B. 80, 105, 110, 119
Rapoport, L. 51, 52
regression 40, 42, 127
Robinson, D. 17
Roche, E. 51
roles 46, 51, 55
Rutter, M. 34, 75

Salzberger-Wittenberg, I.   41
Saunders, C.   18, 20
Schiff, M. S.   29, 121, 123
Schowalter, J. E.   35
Schutz, A. and Luckmann, T.   74
Schwab, J. J. *et al.*   28
self-knowledge   56—9, 85, 88
Sheldon, B.   5, 12
Silverman, P. R.   123
Smith, C. R.   57
social distance   91
social interaction   47—9, 50—3,
    55, 70, 87, 88, 98, 106—10,
    119, 126—8
social networks   35, 50, 64, 110
social withdrawal   20—2, 77, 78,
    83, 86, 87
social work
    conceptualisation   5
    evaluation   6
    knowledge   4, 10—13,
        126—32
    skills   4, 126—32
spiritual help   84
Stacey, M. *et al.*   17

Steele, D. W.   113
stillbirth   50
Stockwell, F.   65
Strauss, A. L. and Glaser, B. G.
    14, 18
subjective reality   46, 47
Sudnow, D.   18
symbolic interactionism   48
systems theory   5, 6

Tallmer, M.   35
terminal care   15, 16
Tessler, R. C.   58
Timms, N. and Timms, R.   10,
    11, 12, 56, 127

Volkan, V. D.   33
Volkan, V. D. and Showalter, C. R.
    33
Vollman, R. R. *et al.*   23, 26

Williams, W. V. *et al.*   23

Yamamoto, J. *et al.*   49